I0391169

Christmas Critters

AN ADULT COLOURING BOOK

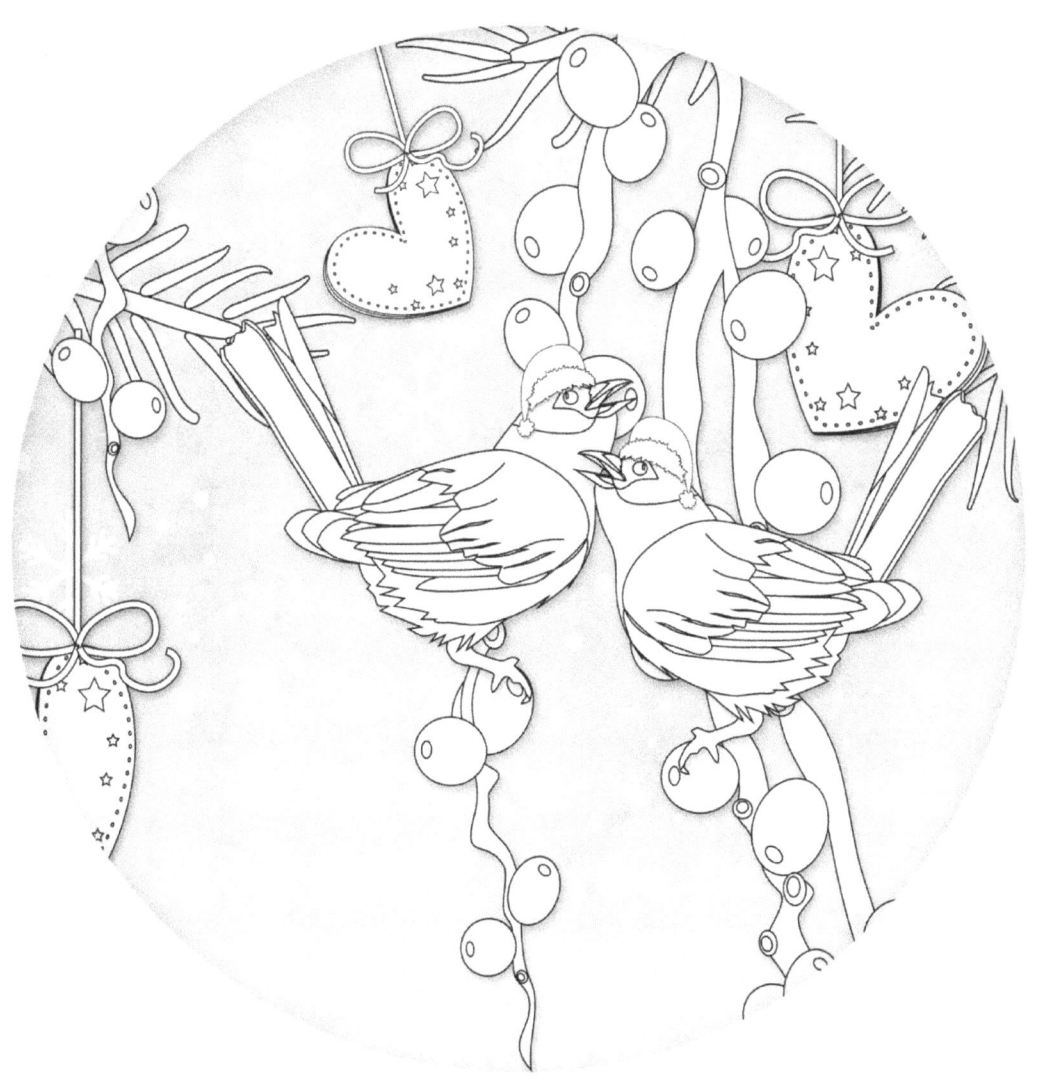

by Lesley Smitheringale

legal

About the Artist

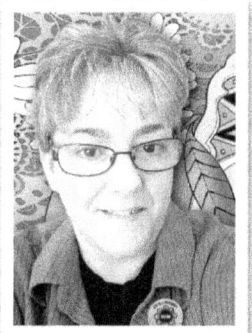

Lesley lives and works in her home studio in the Redlands area of Queensland, Australia. She was born in Glasgow, Scotland where she obtained a BA with Honours in Design at Glasgow School of Art. She then did further training to become an art teacher and after teaching for twenty years to Middle and High School students, Lesley took the plunge and decided to work for herself. She currently teaches extra-curricular art to children, produces her own artwork, hand-made gifts, illustrates and self-publishes art & craft books.

Keep up-to-date

If you love to colour and tangle, Lesley also runs a website and online Shop at Colouring and Tangling where she offers inspiration, tips & techniques, video instruction and a large range of products such as books, printable pdfs, Calendars, Cards, Bookmarks, Artist Prints and Giftware for colourists and lovers of zentangle-inspired art. Why not visit and sign up for Lesley's Newsletter and keep up-to-date?

Lesley also hosts a private Facebook Group which fans and colourists of her illustrations can join, offering you the opportunity to showcase your colourings from any of her books and products, meet a creative, virtual community and enjoy giveaways, video instruction and up-to-date news of new colouring resources.

Visit https://www.facebook.com/groups/LesleySmitheringaleArtColouring/ and ask to join!

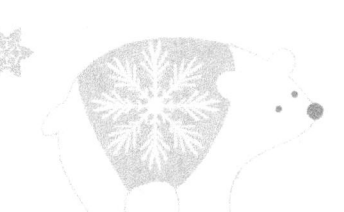

http://www.colouringandtangling.com
https://www.facebook.com/colouringandtangling
https://www.etsy.com/shop/ColouringandTangling

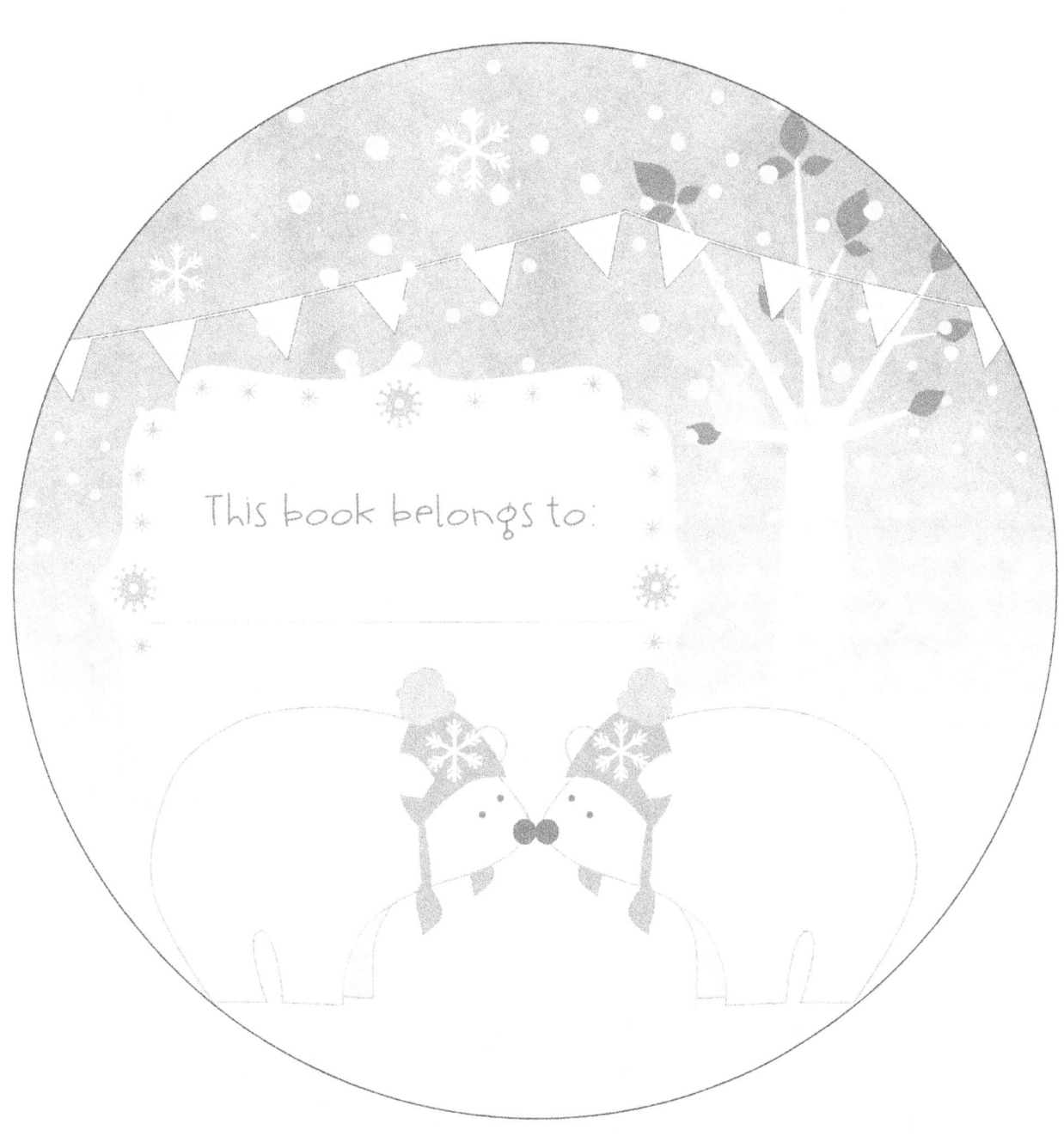

This book belongs to:

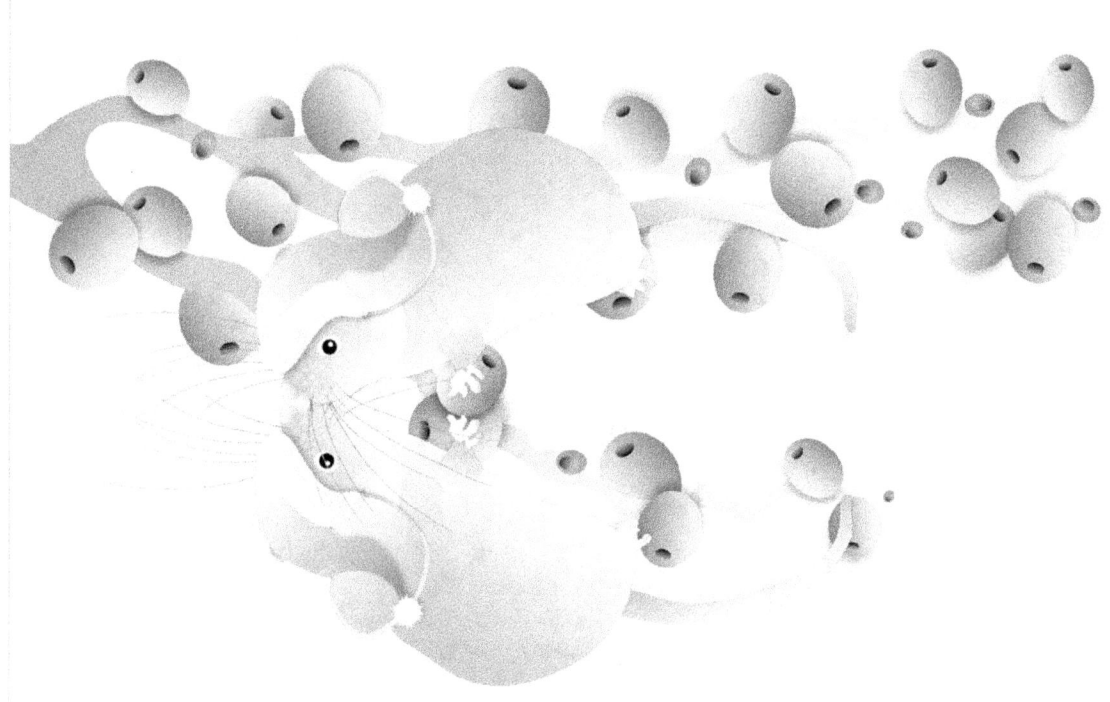
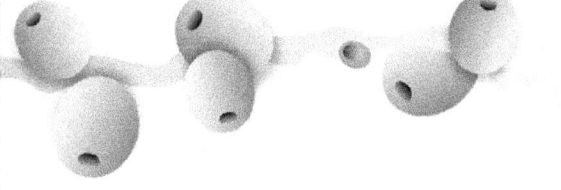

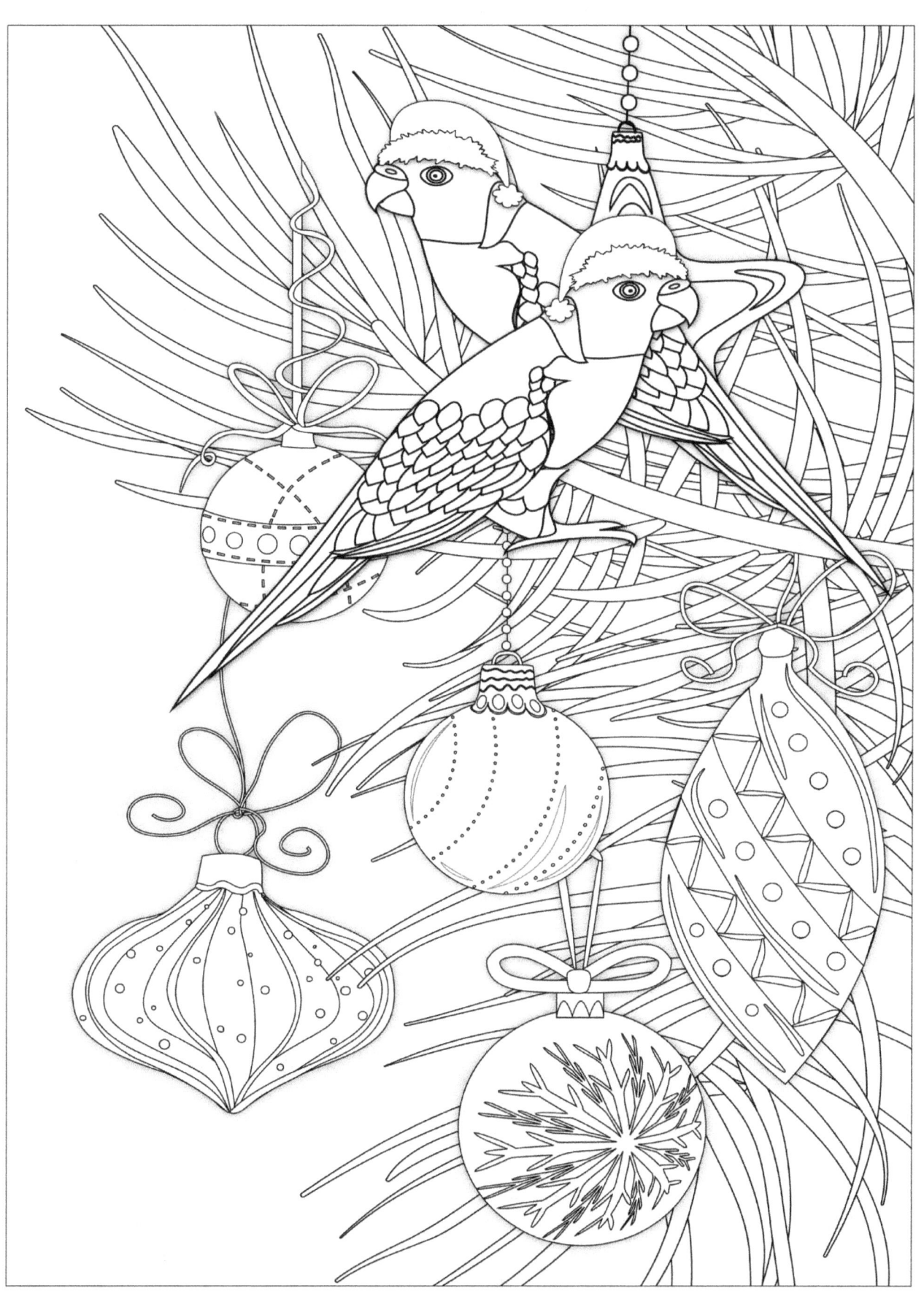

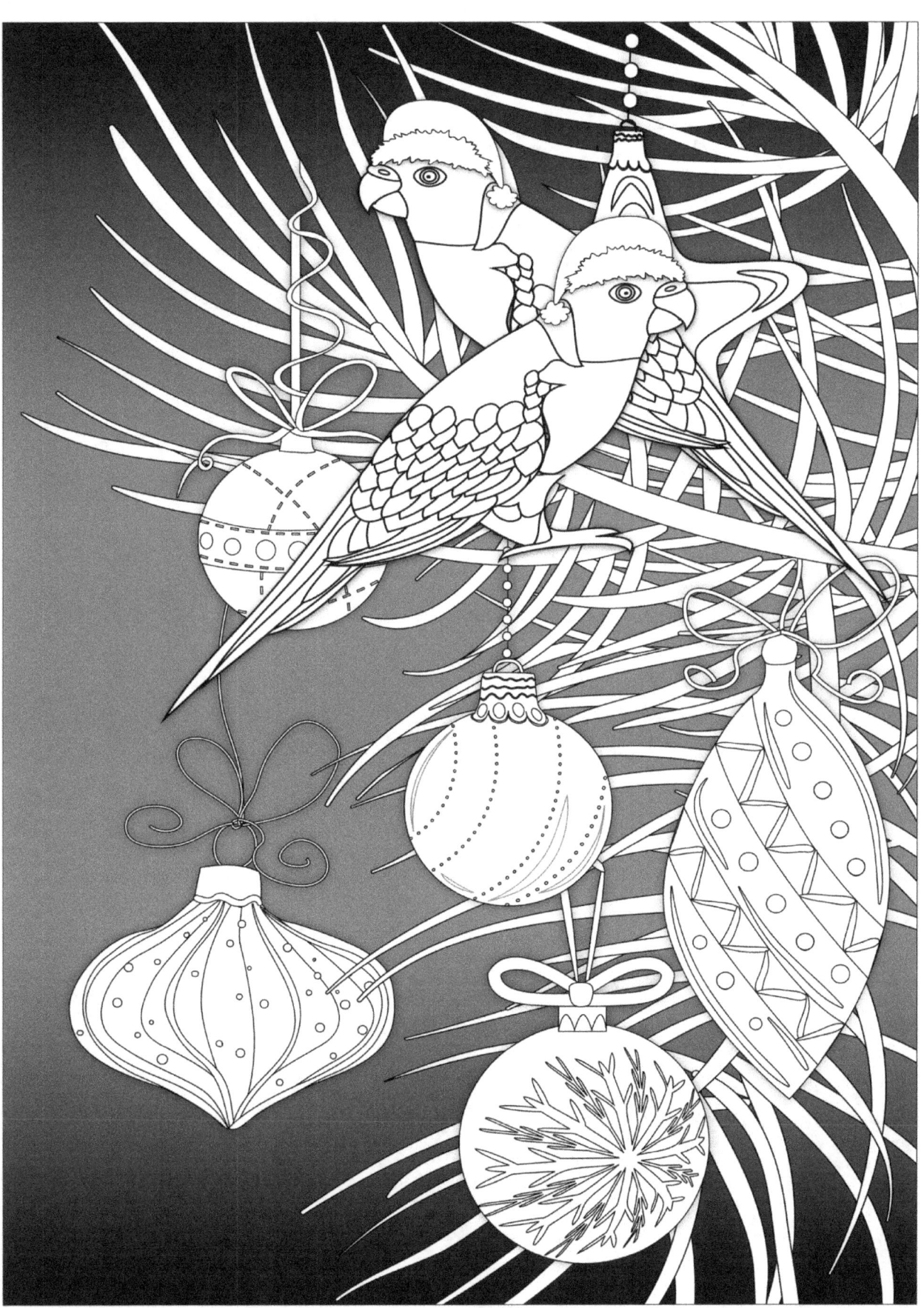

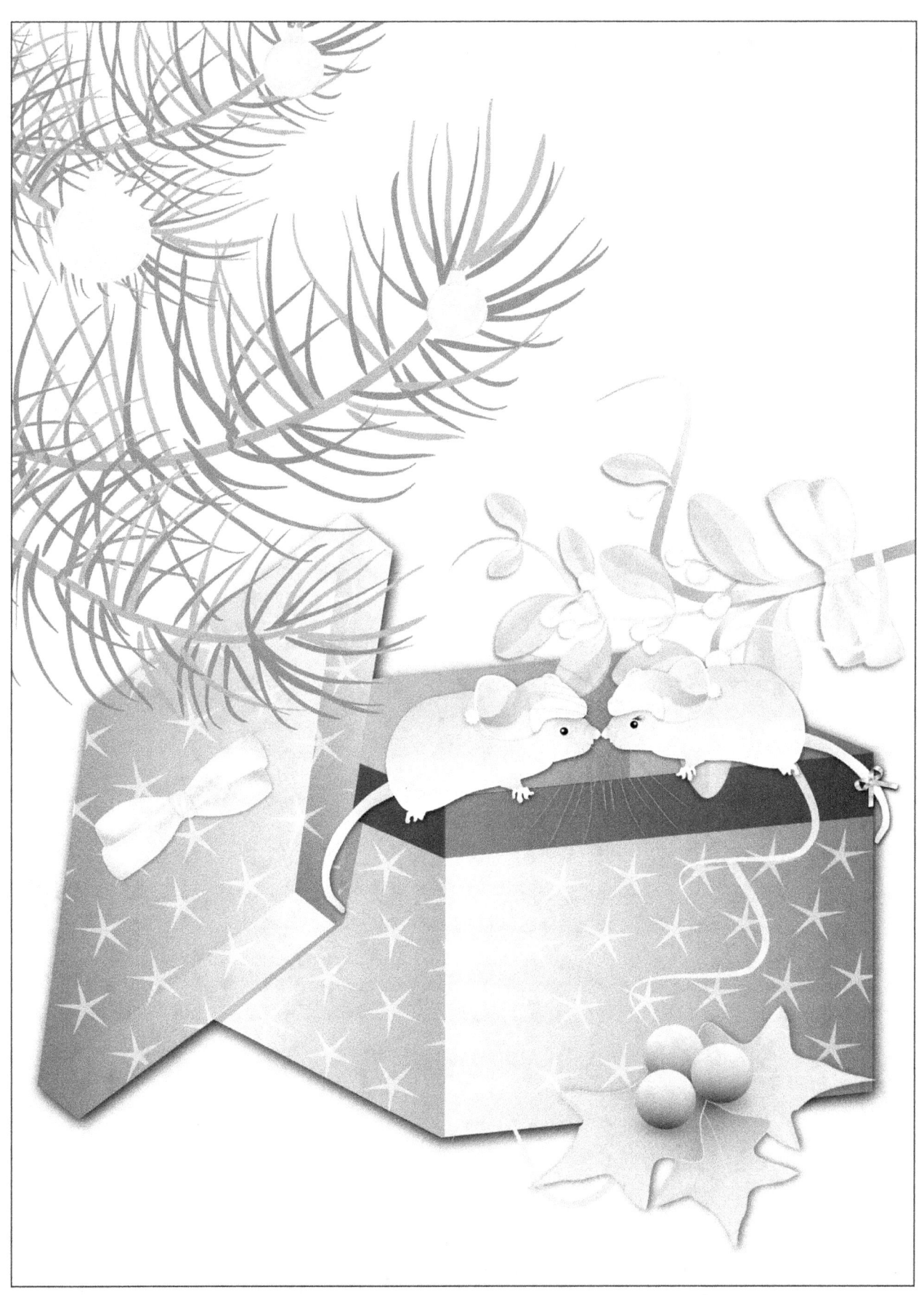

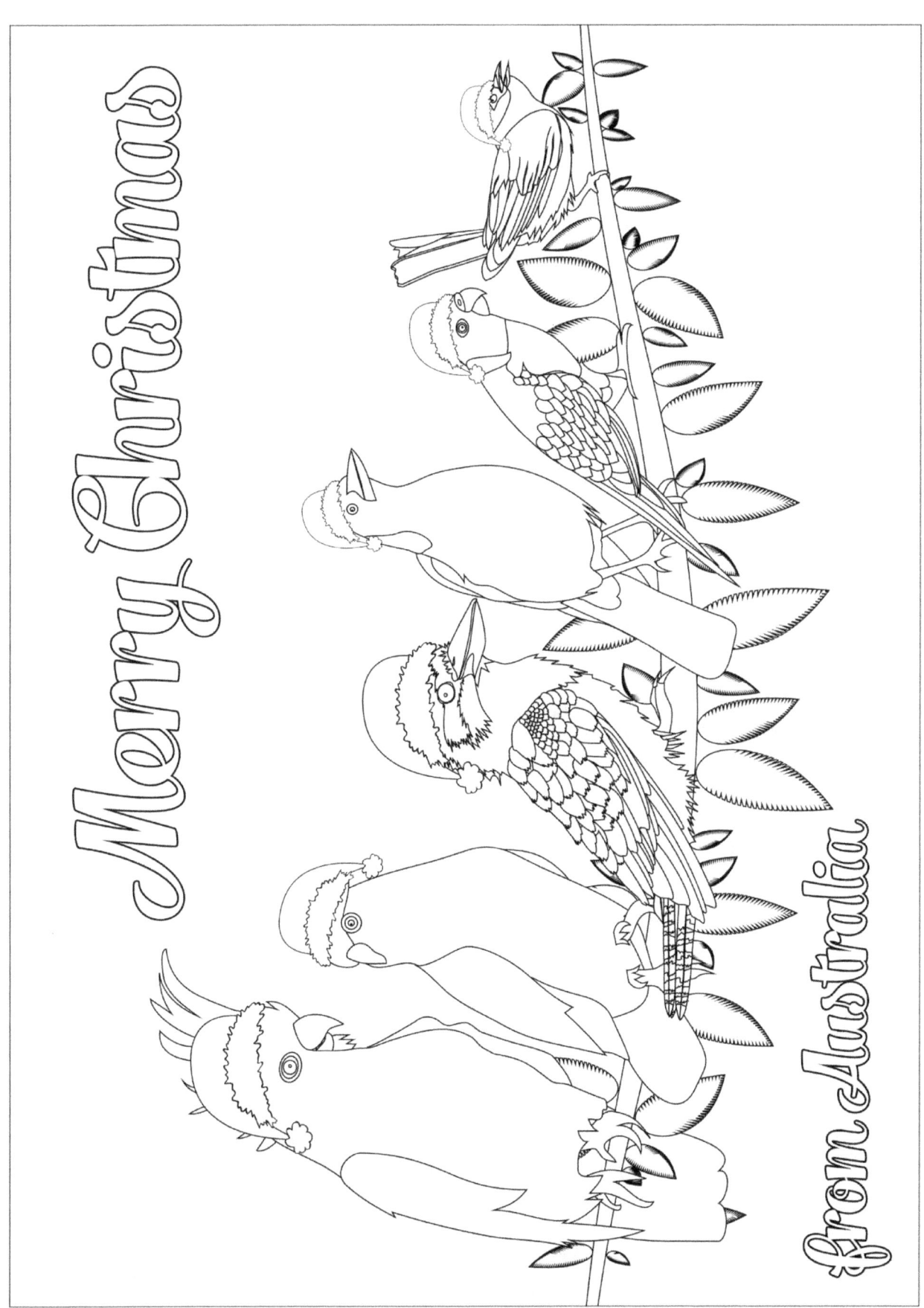

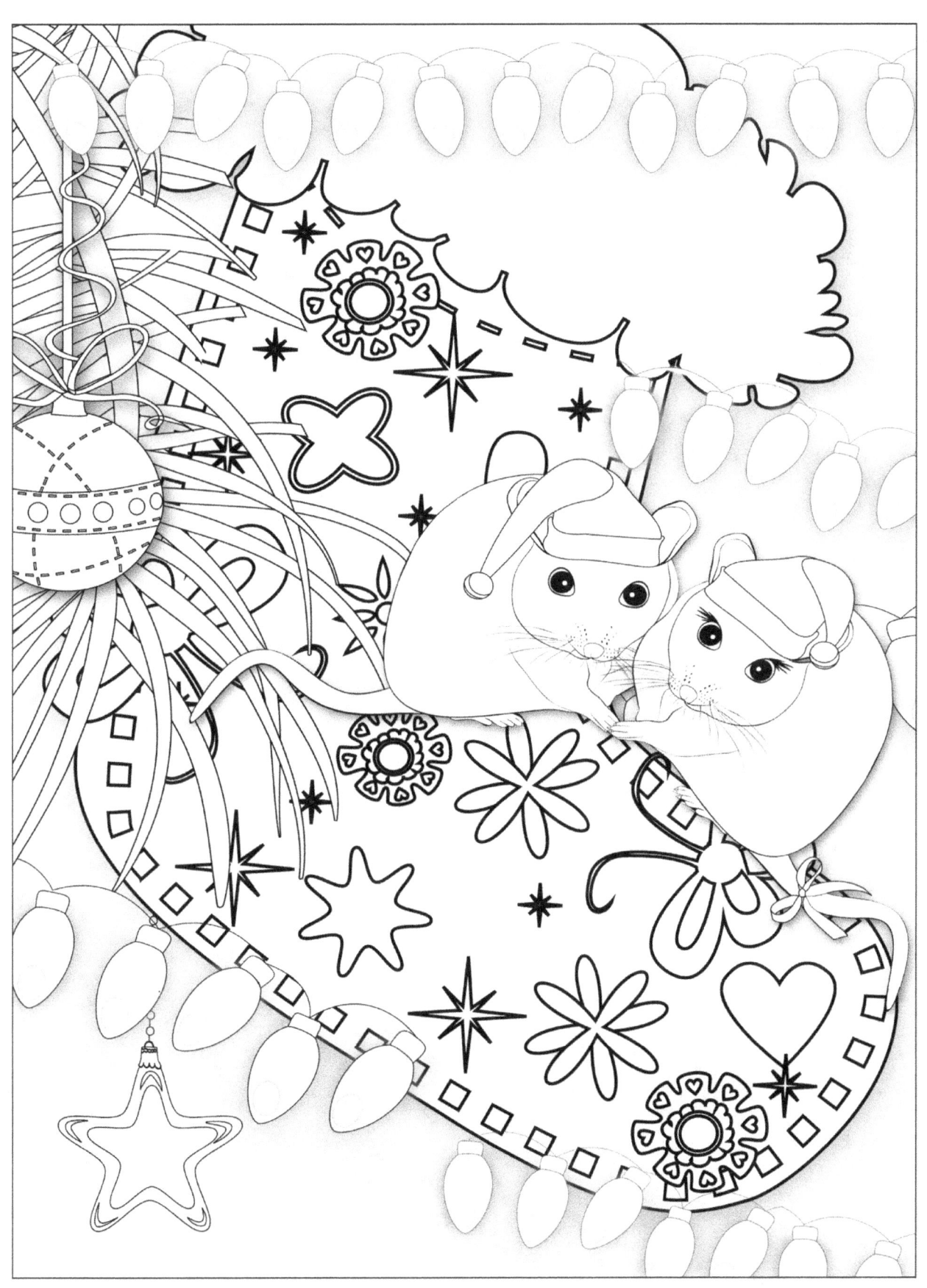

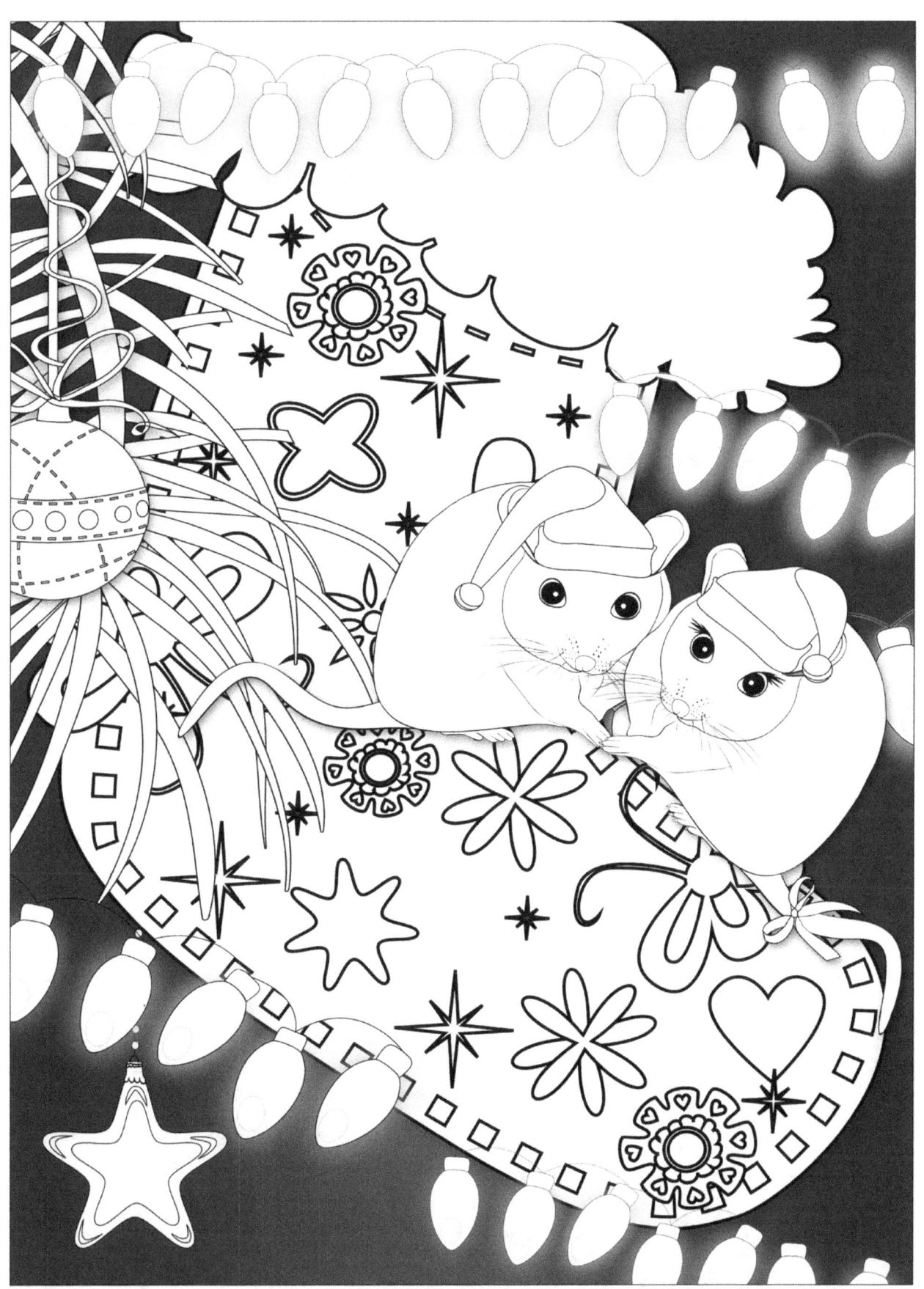

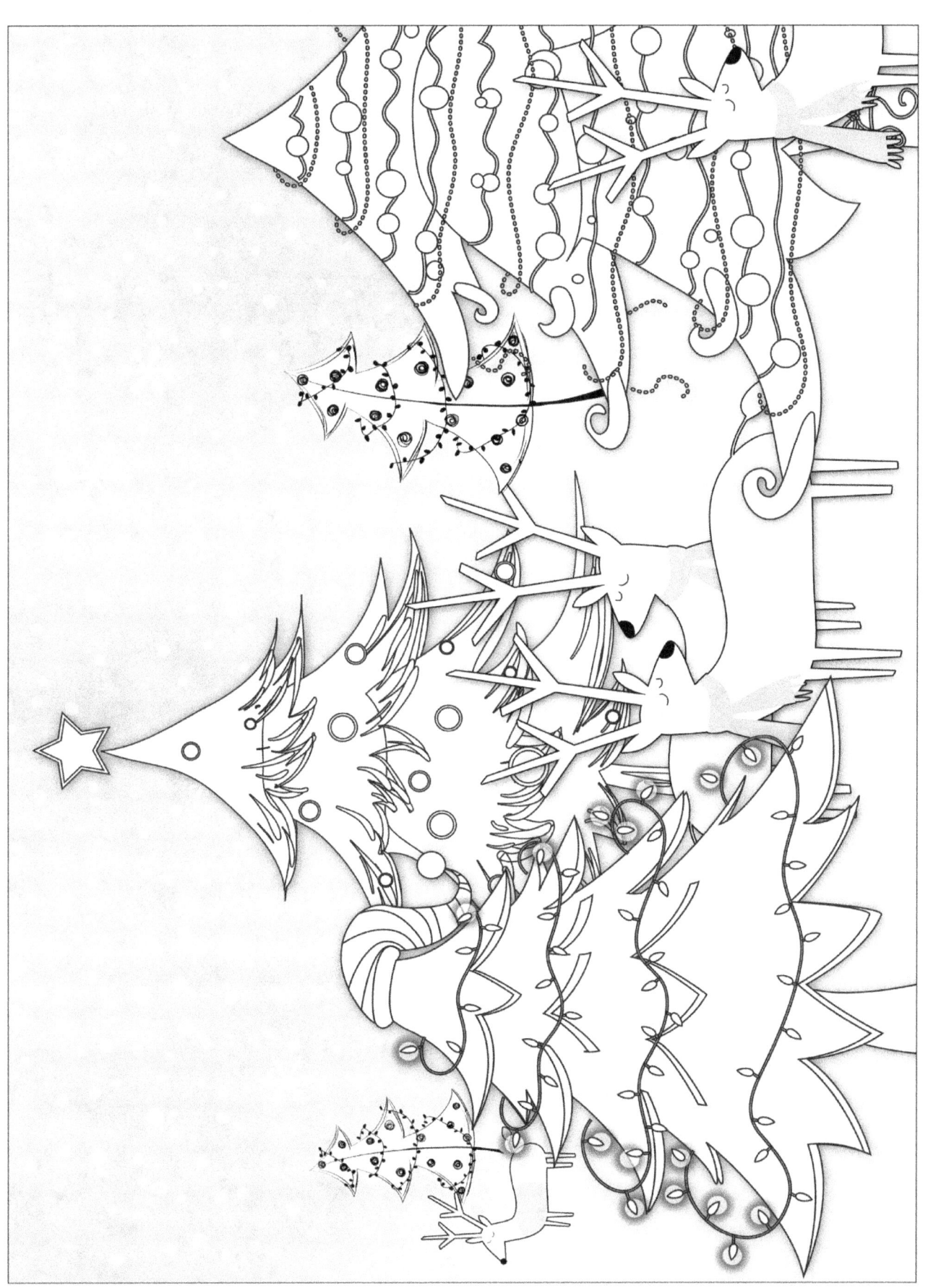

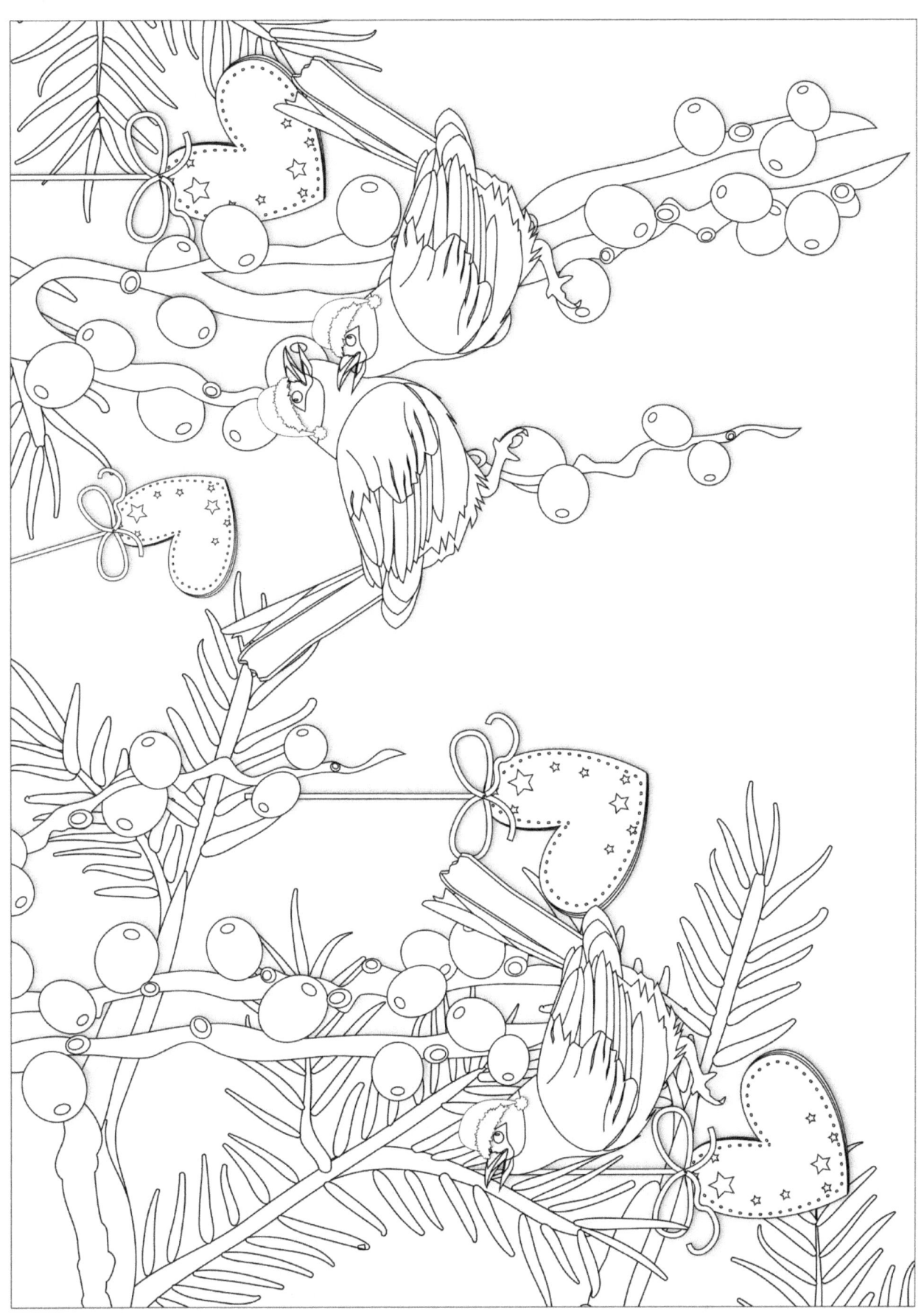

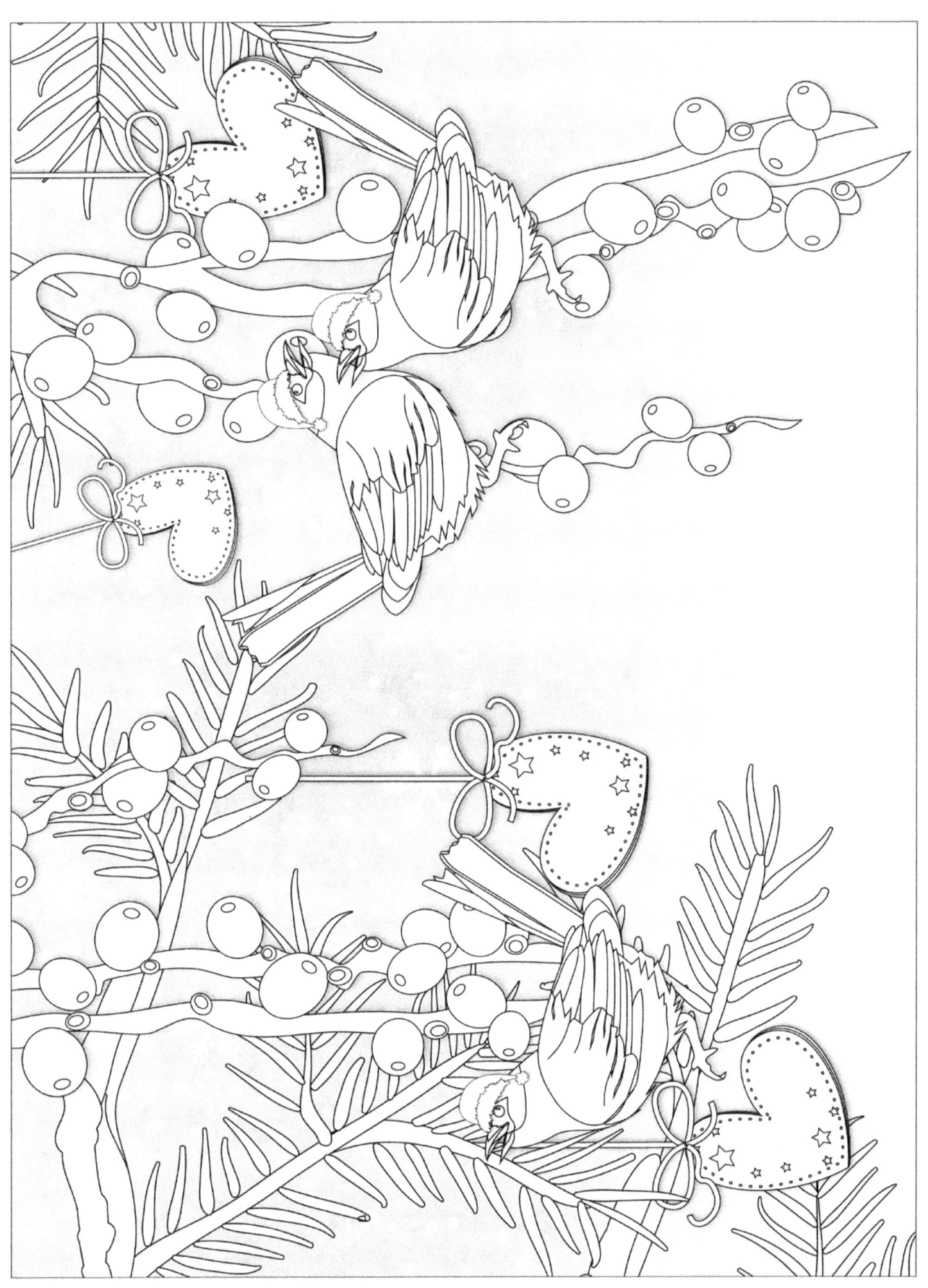

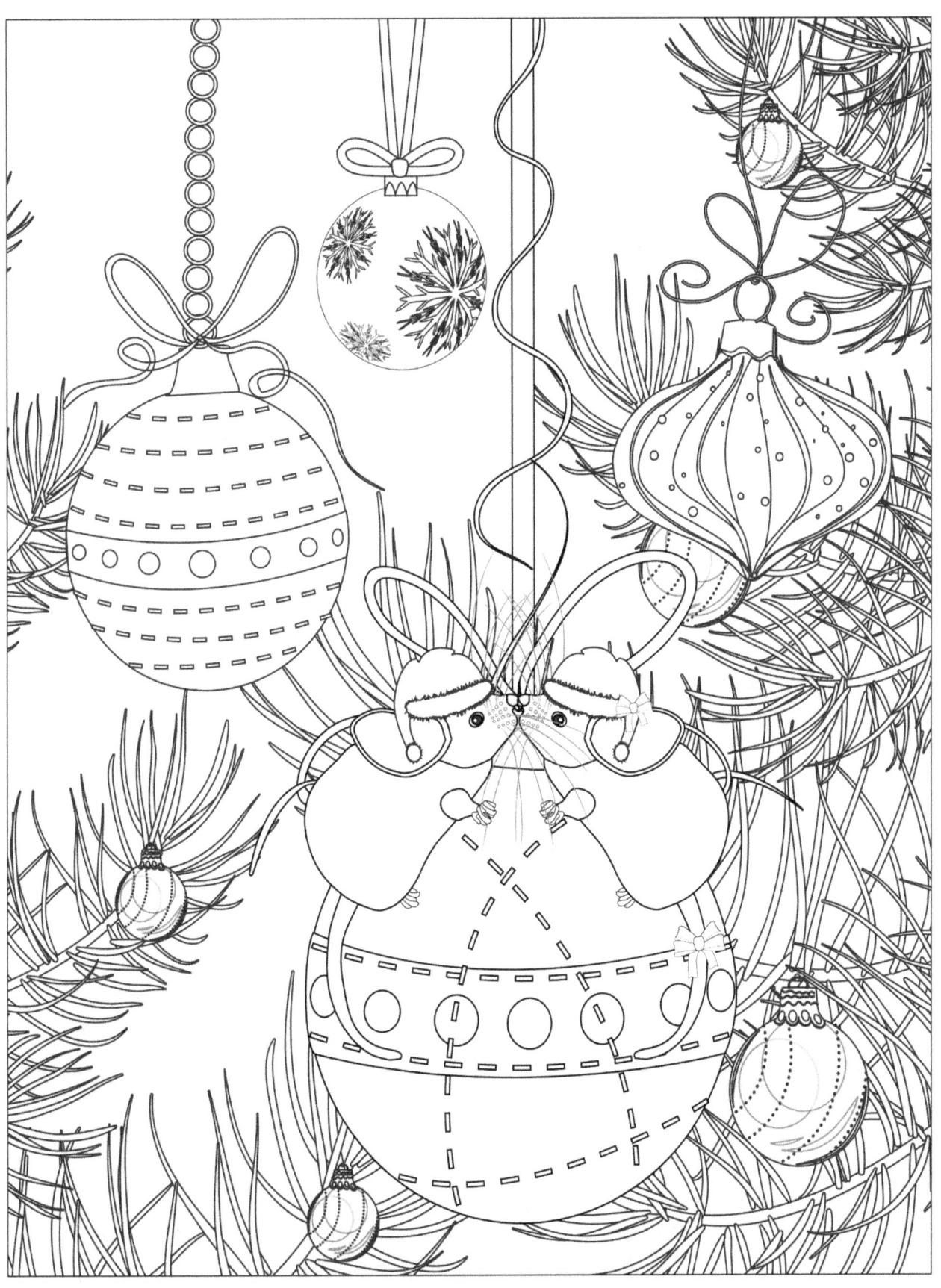

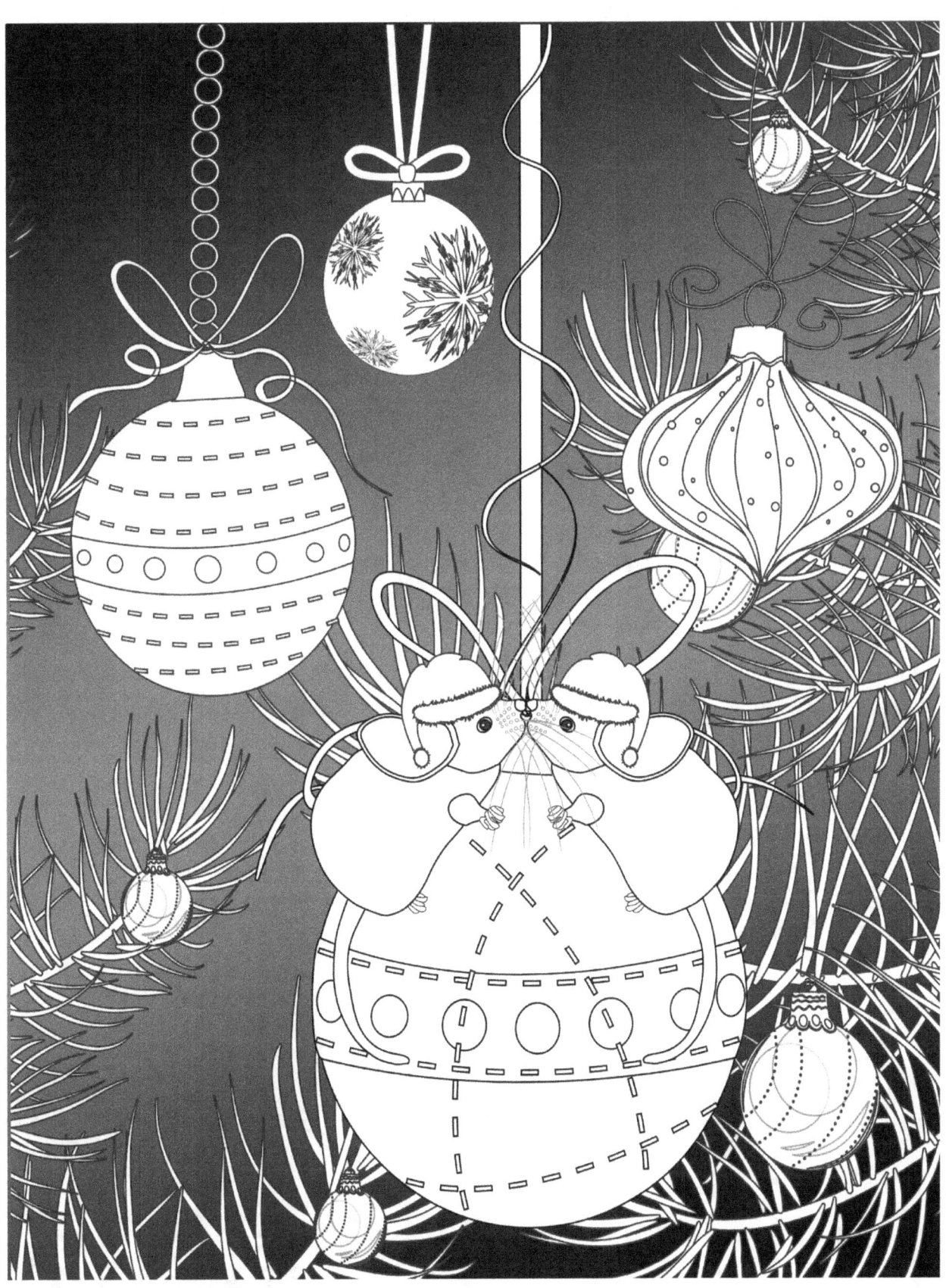

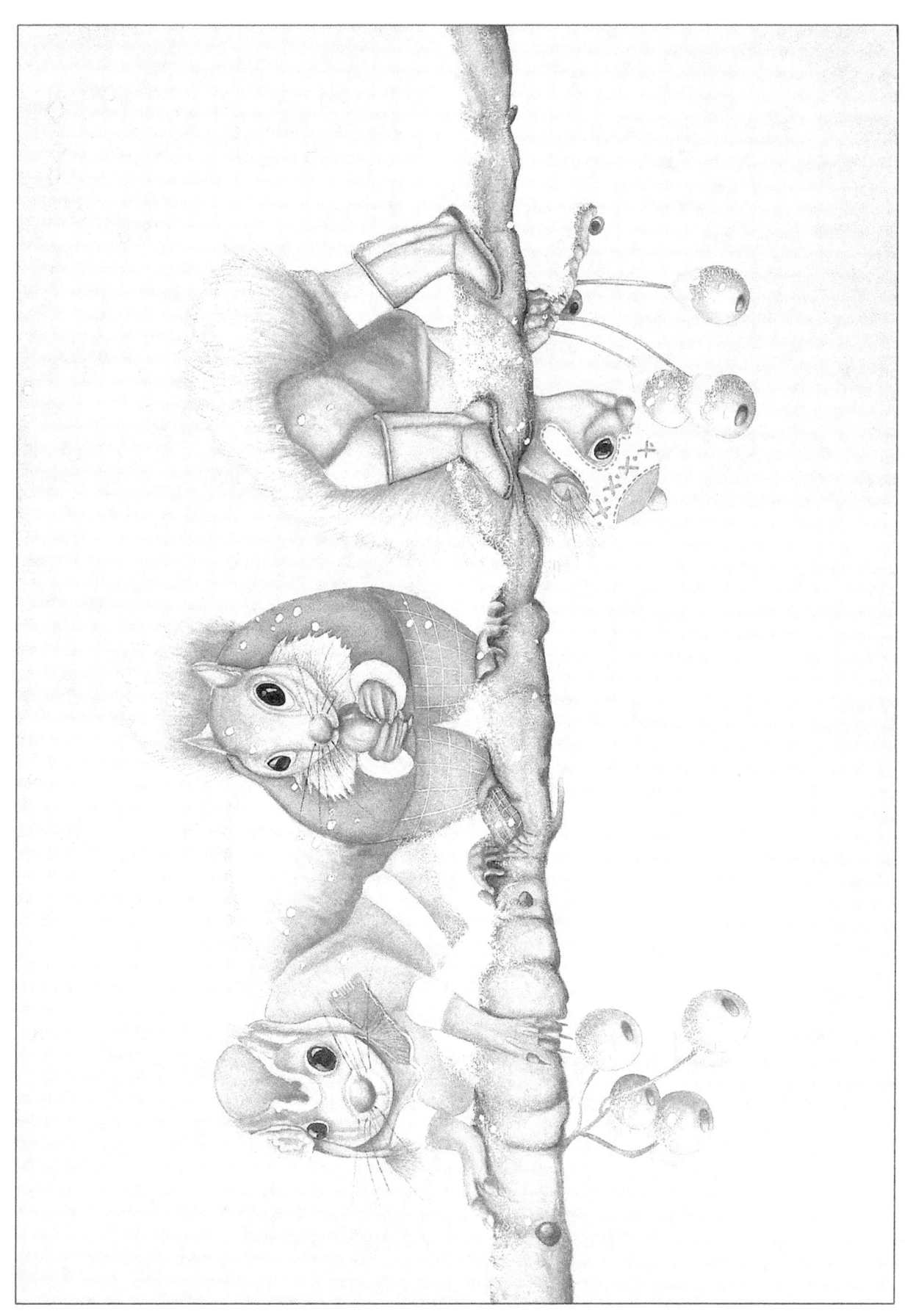

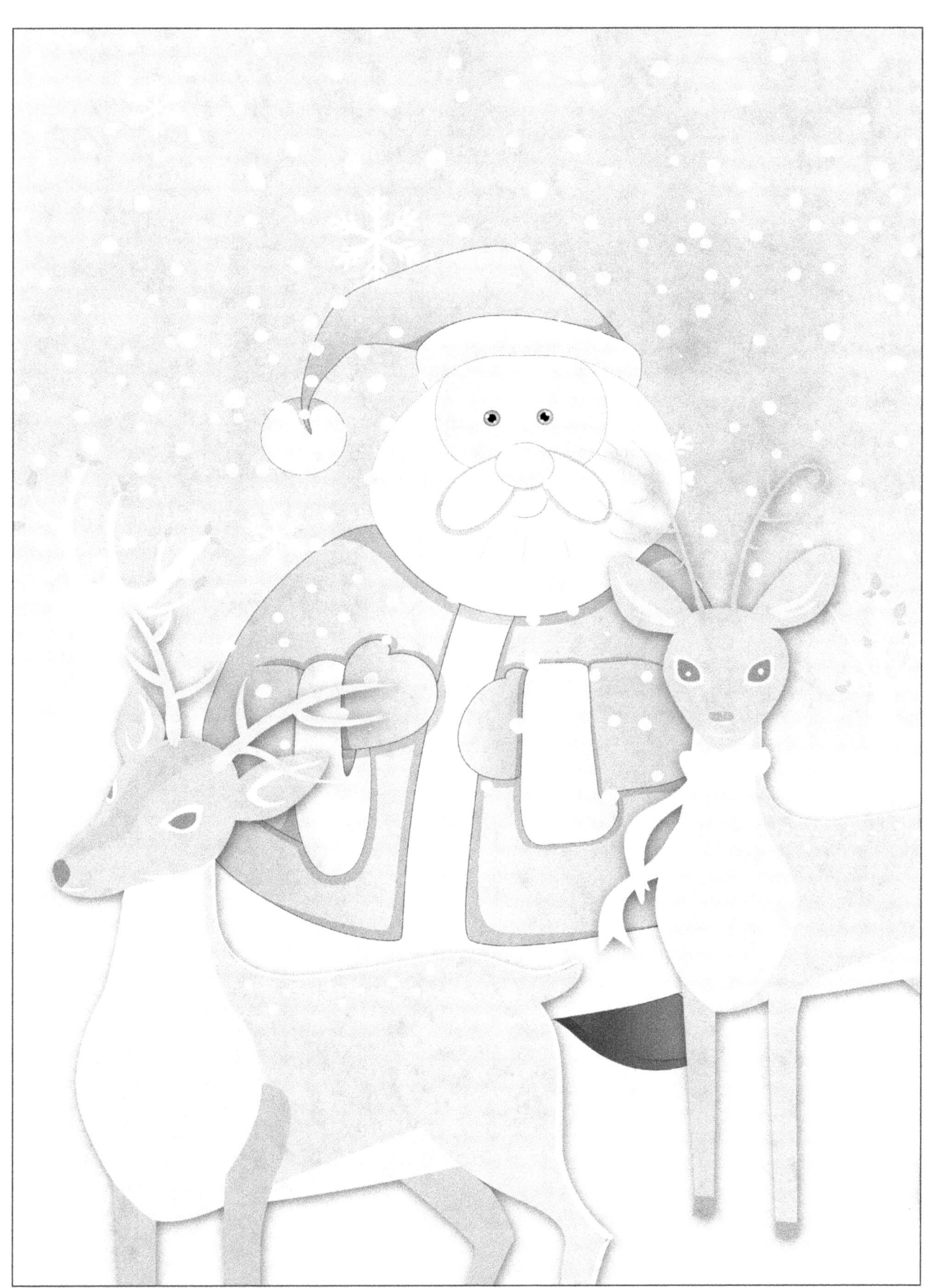

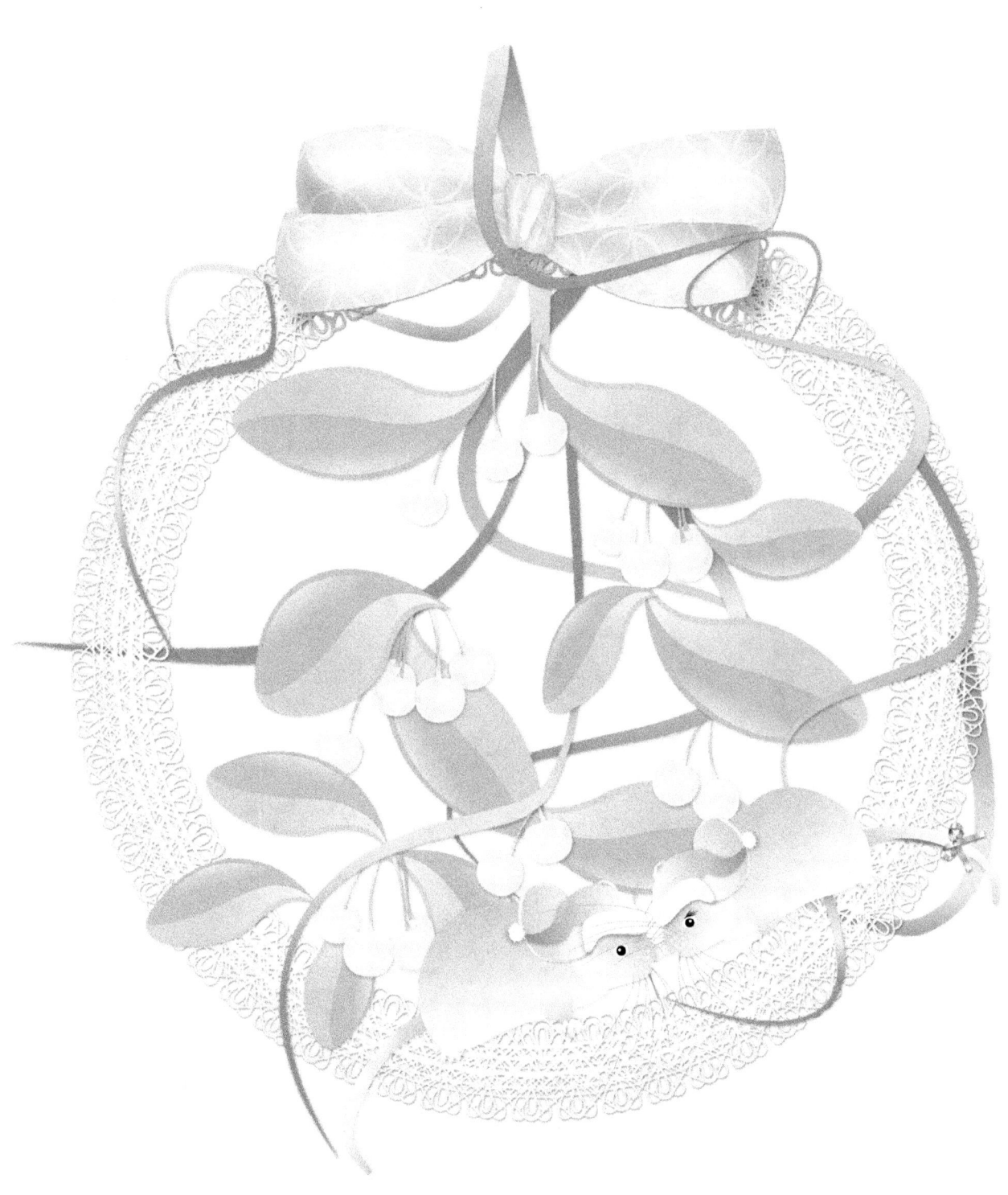

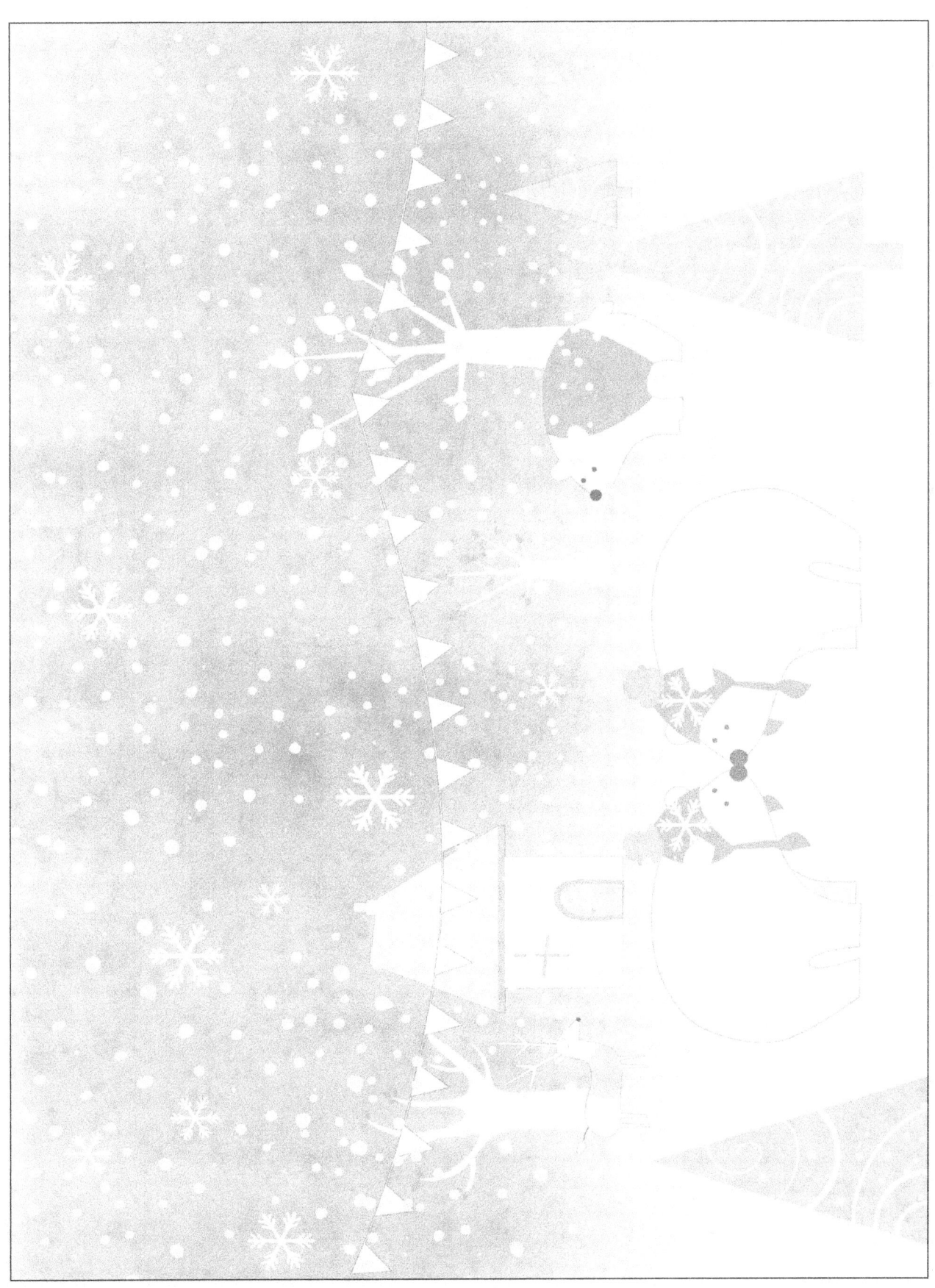

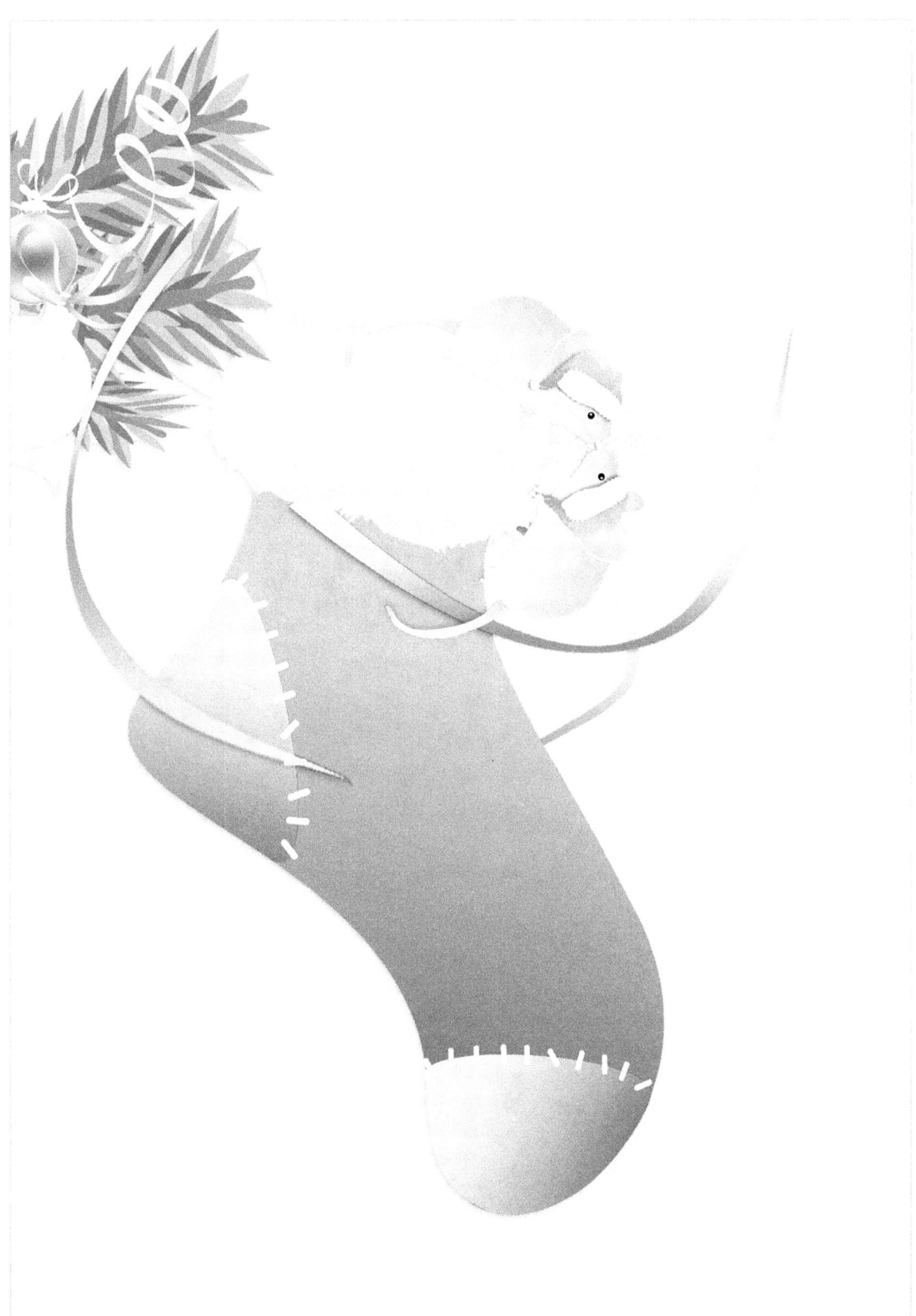

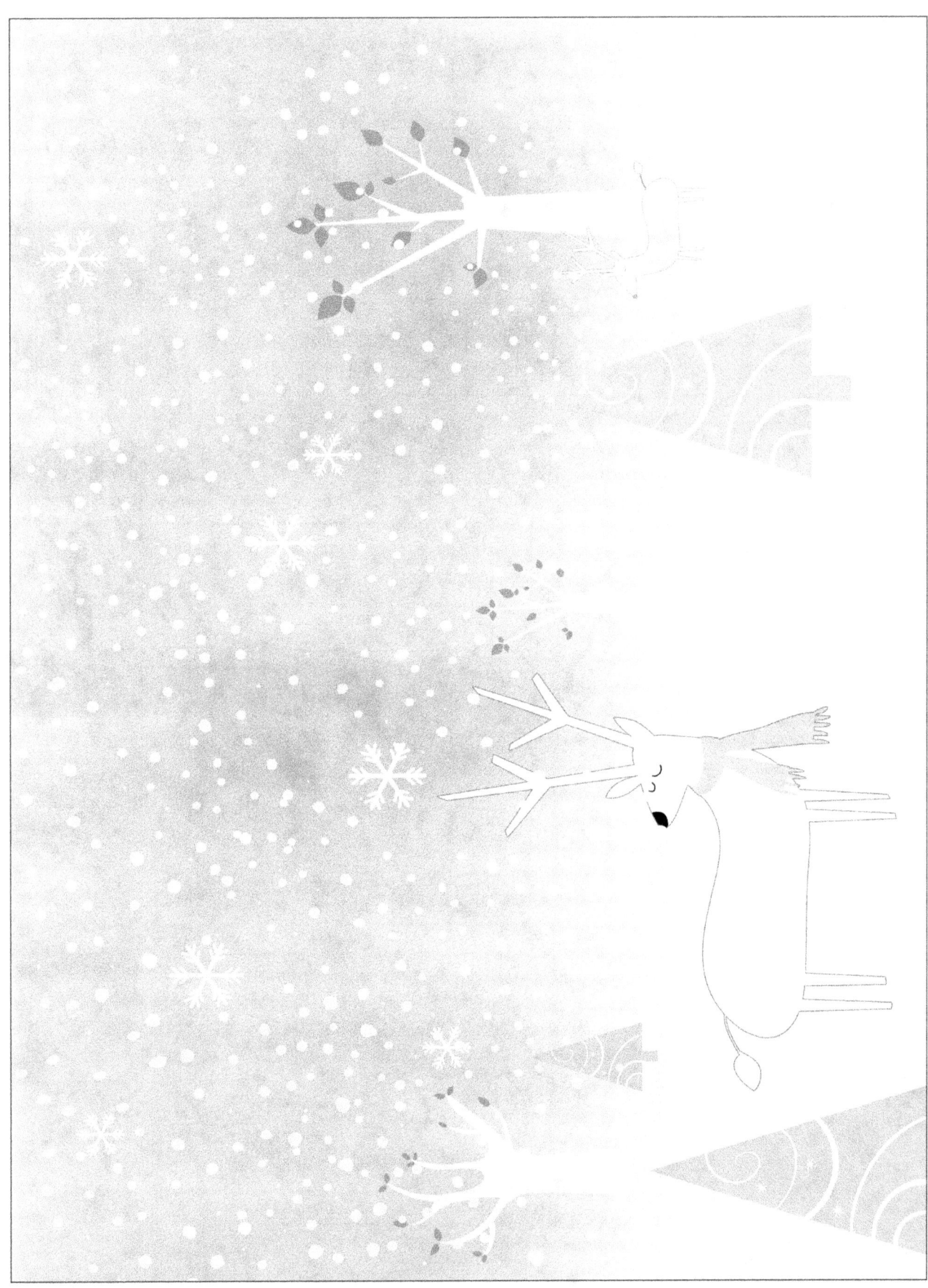

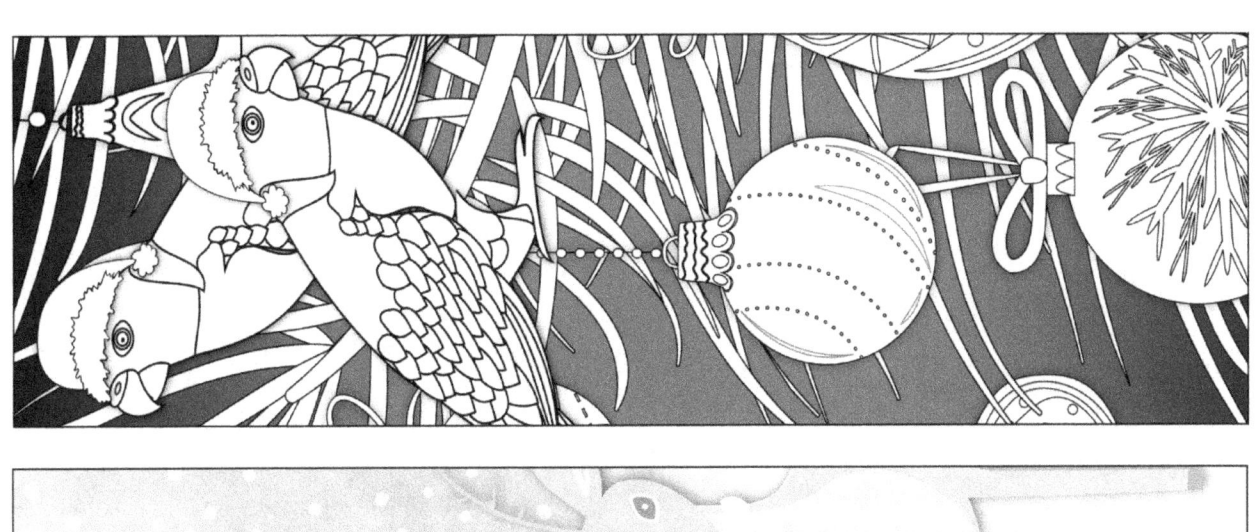

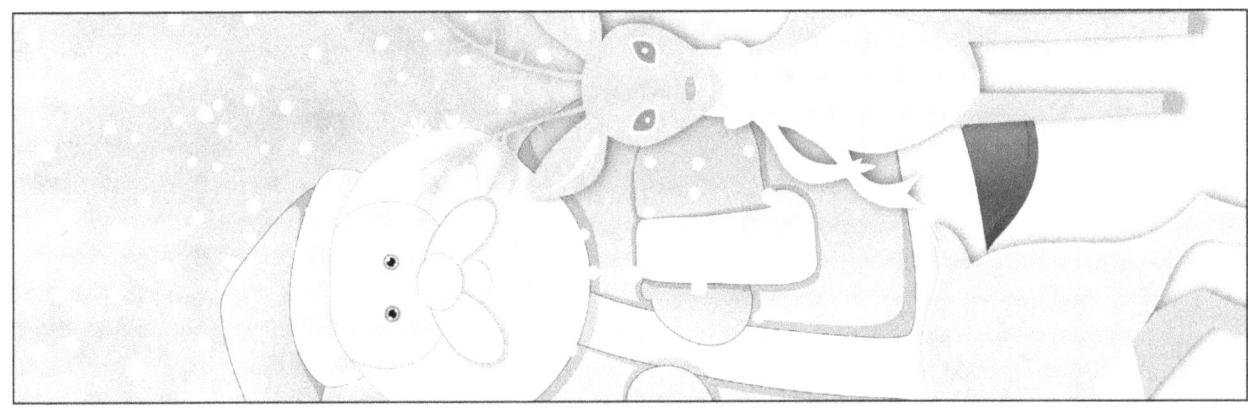

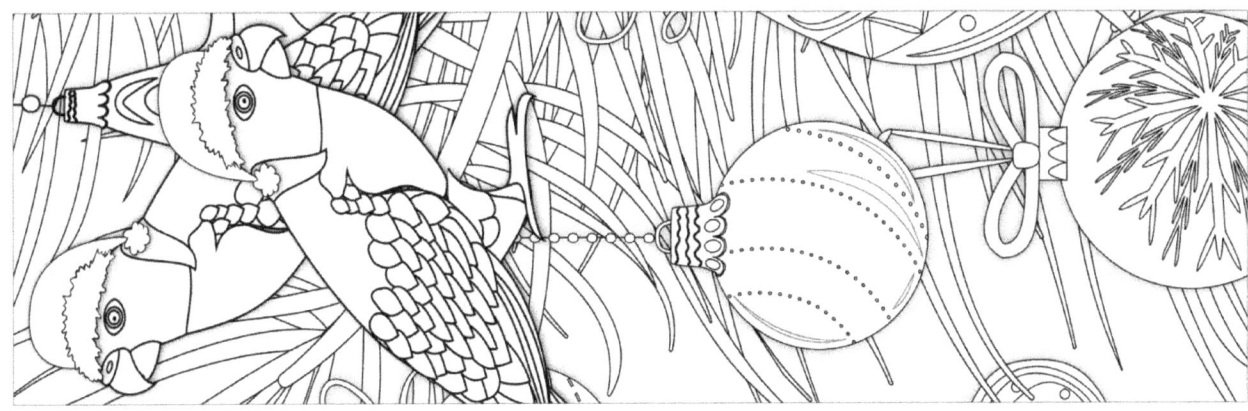

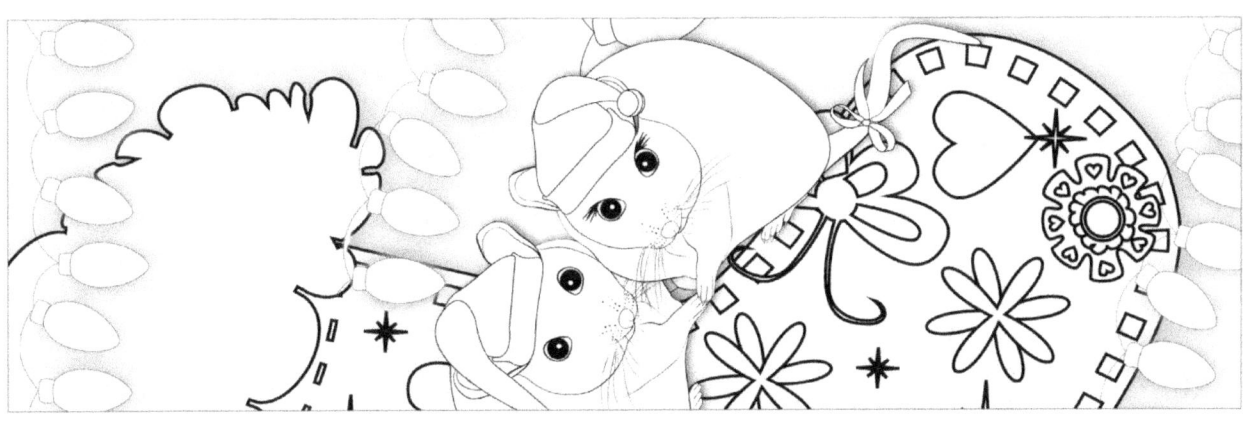

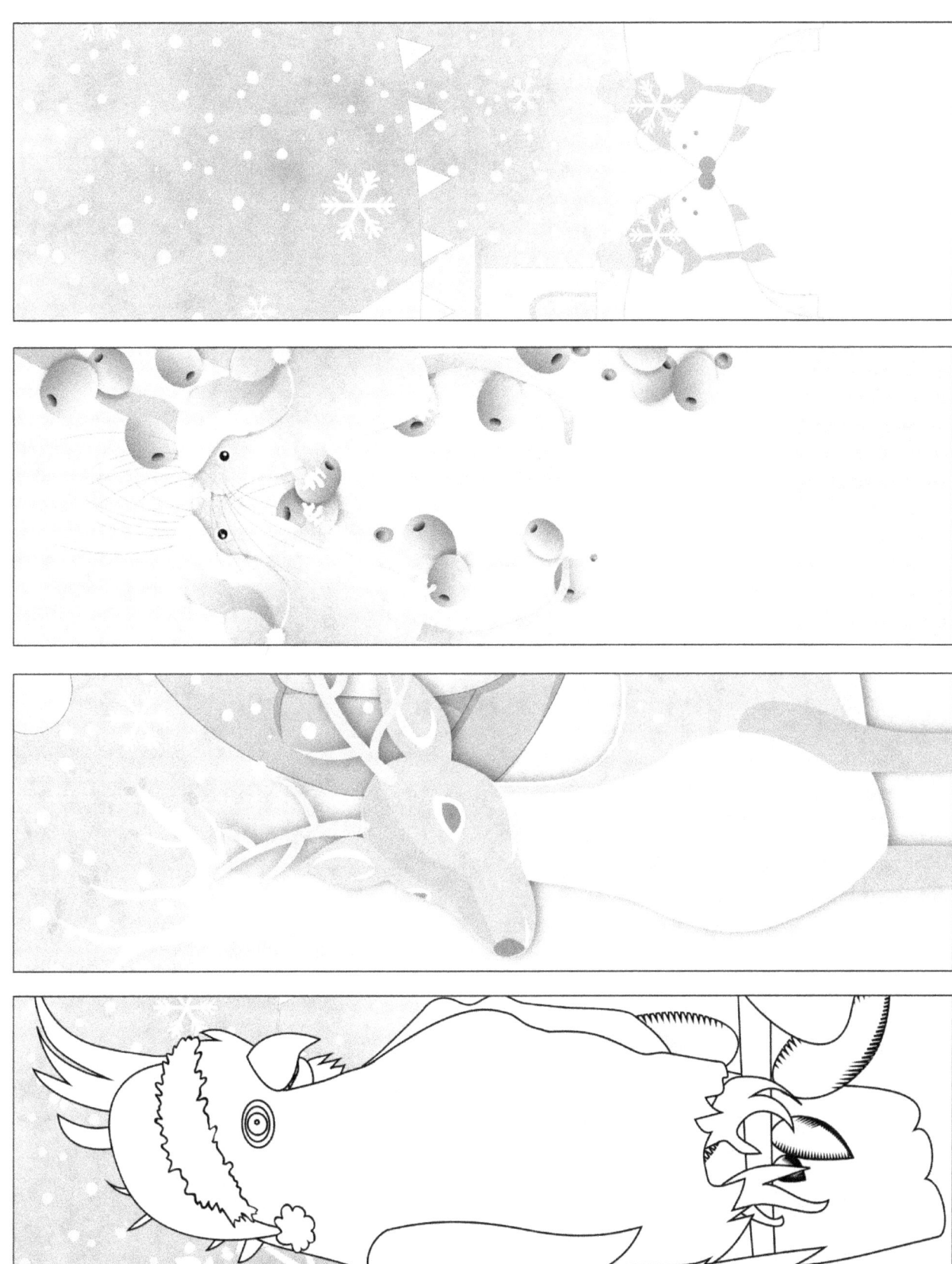

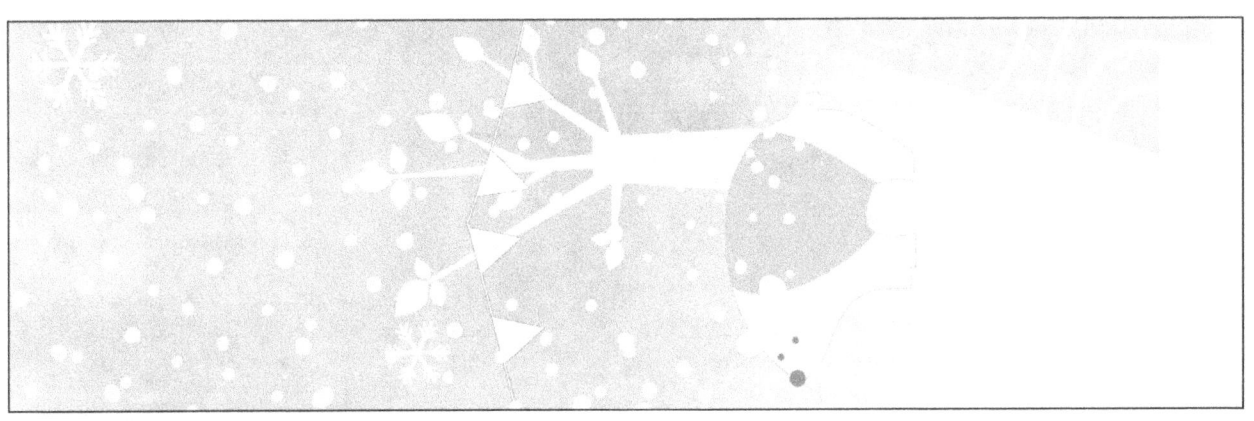

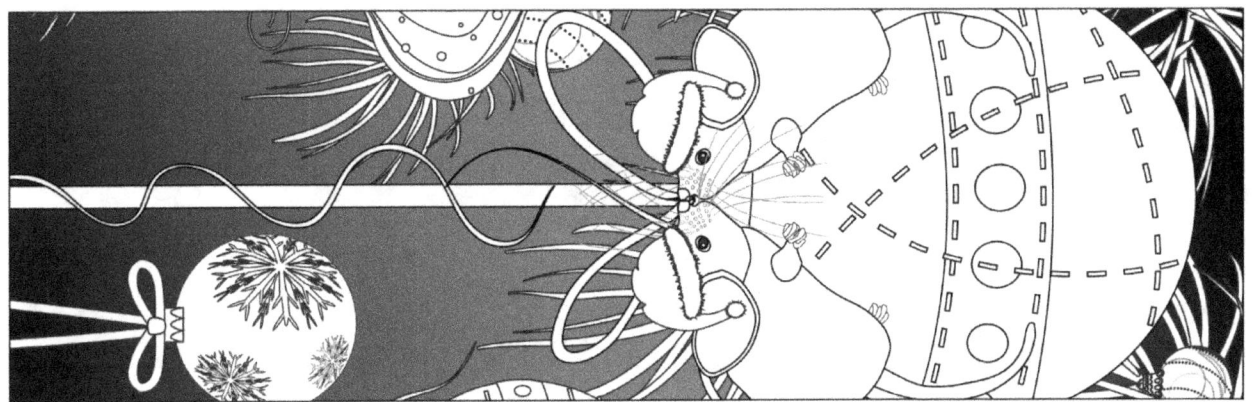

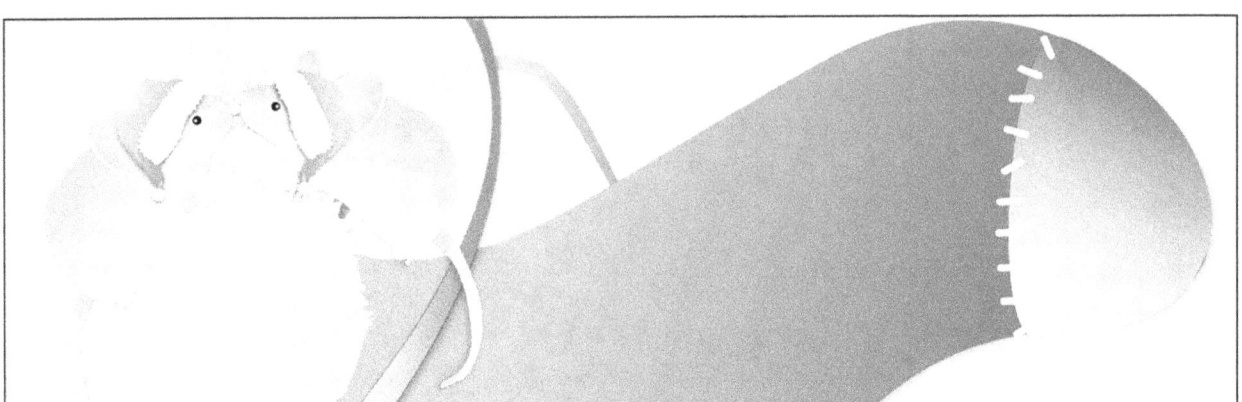

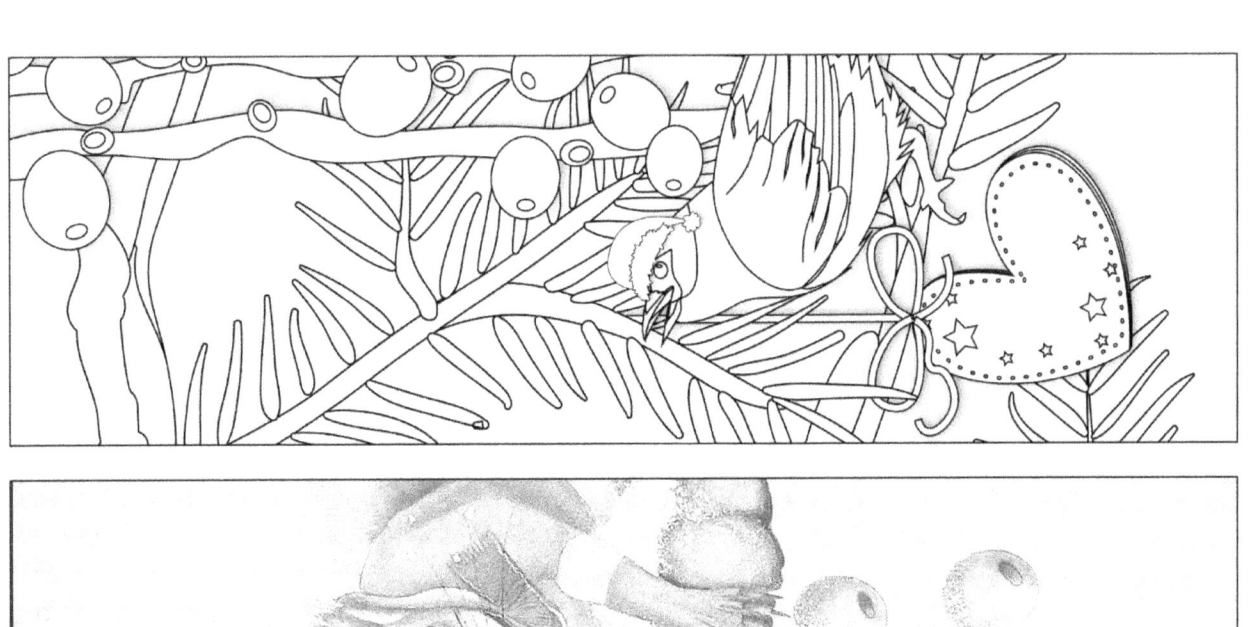

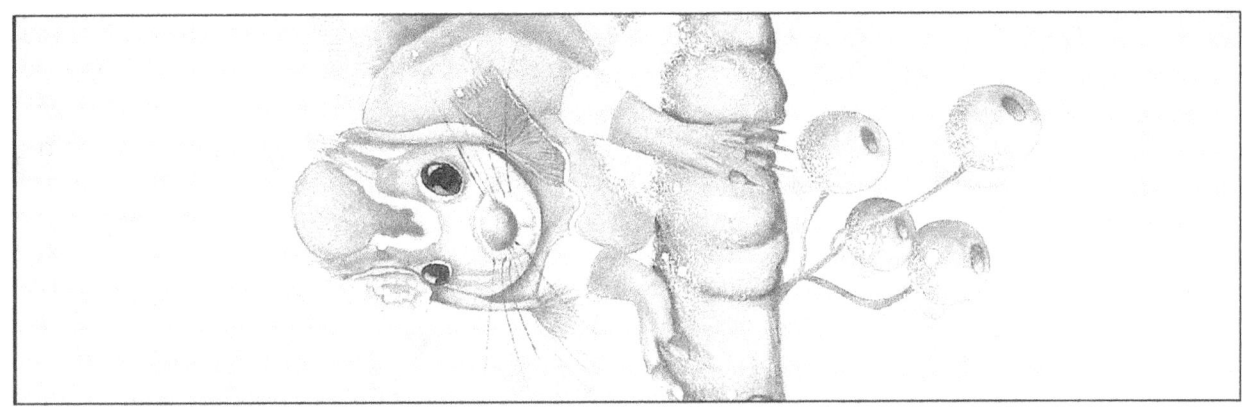

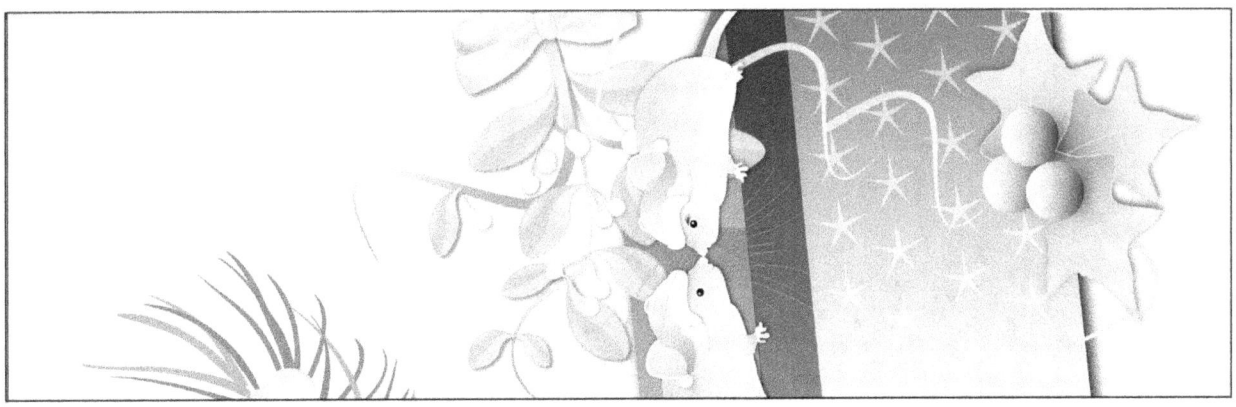

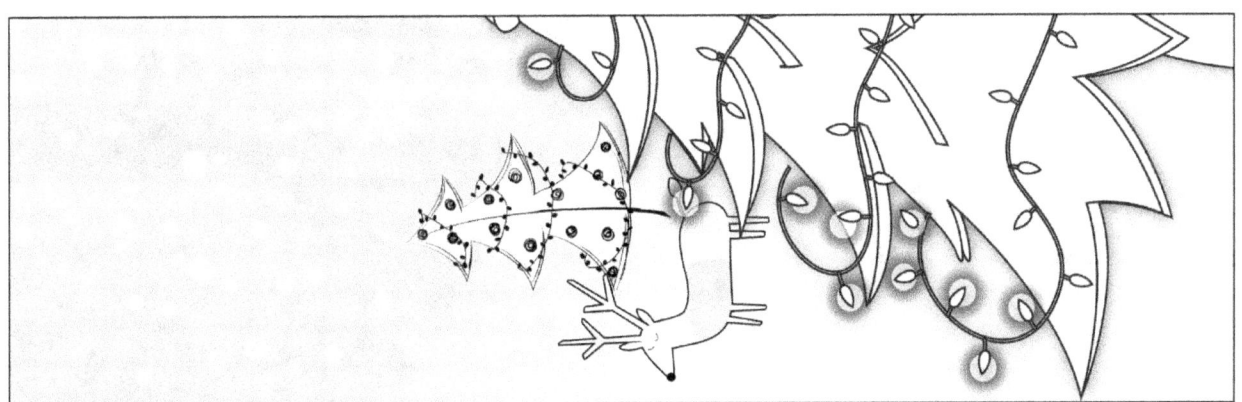

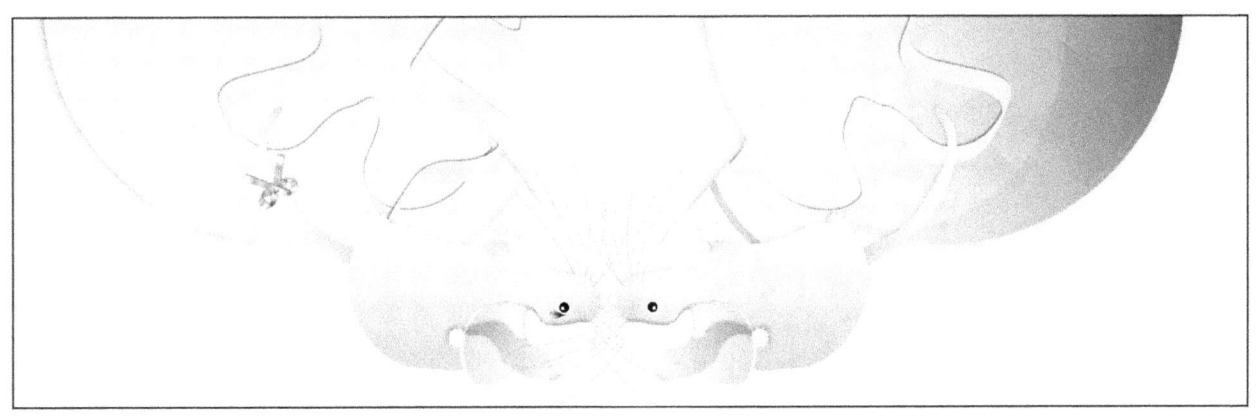

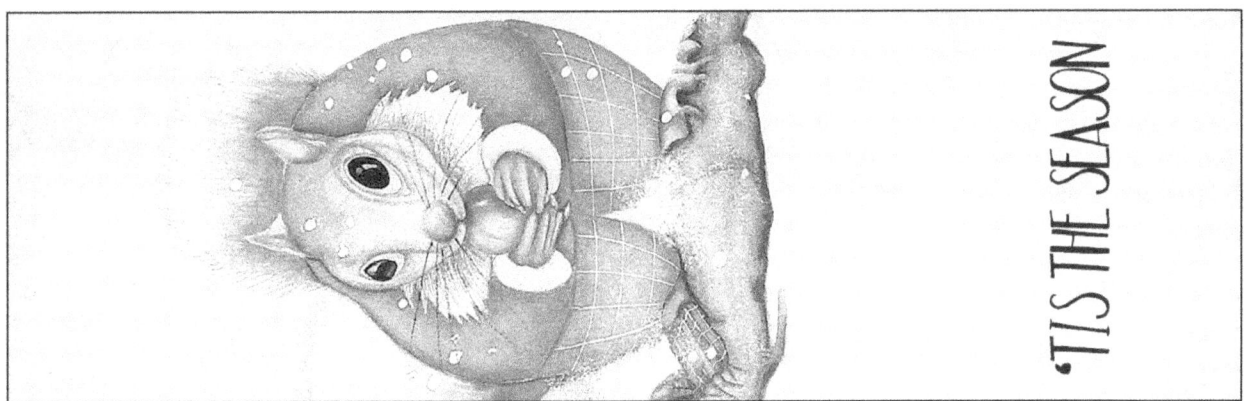

'TIS THE SEASON

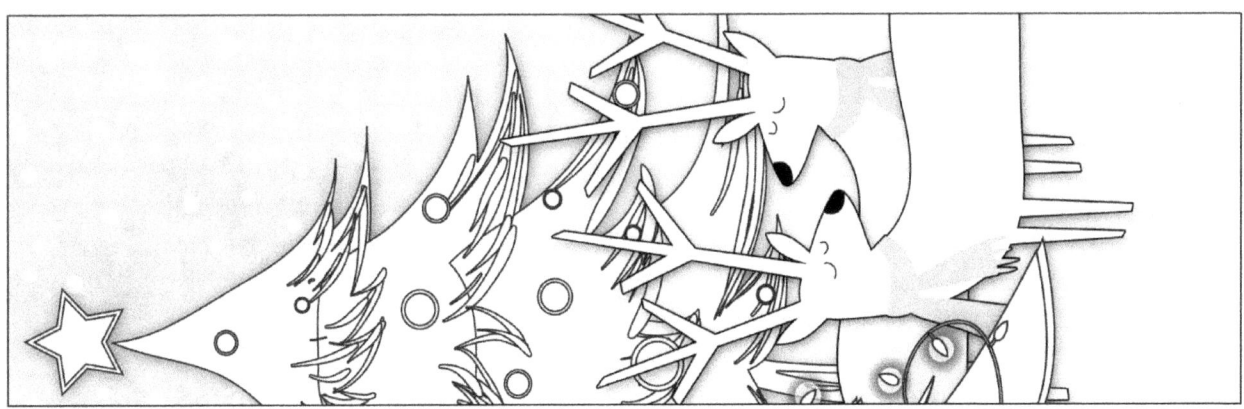

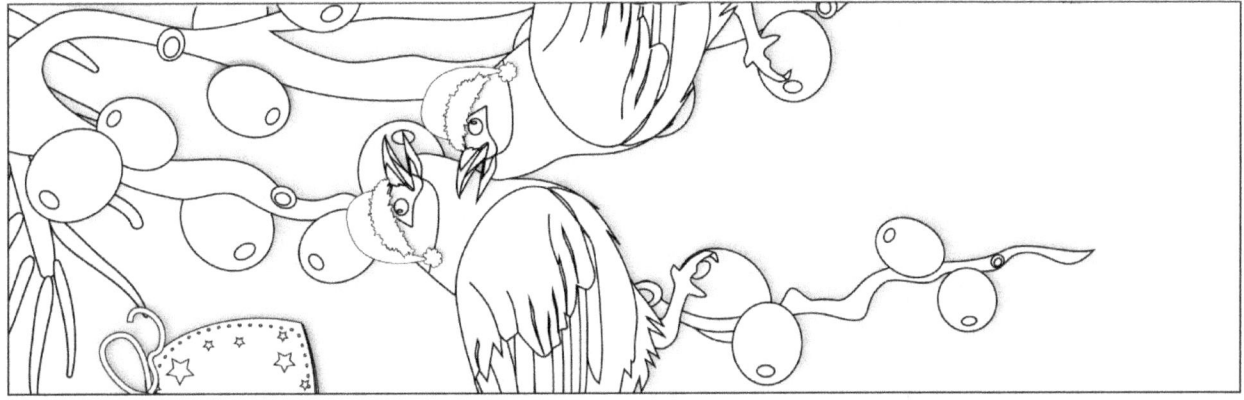

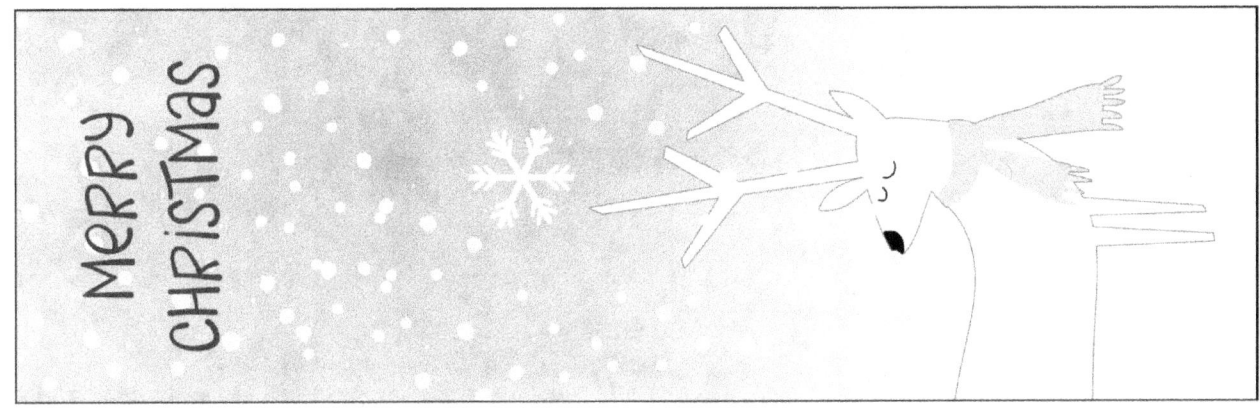

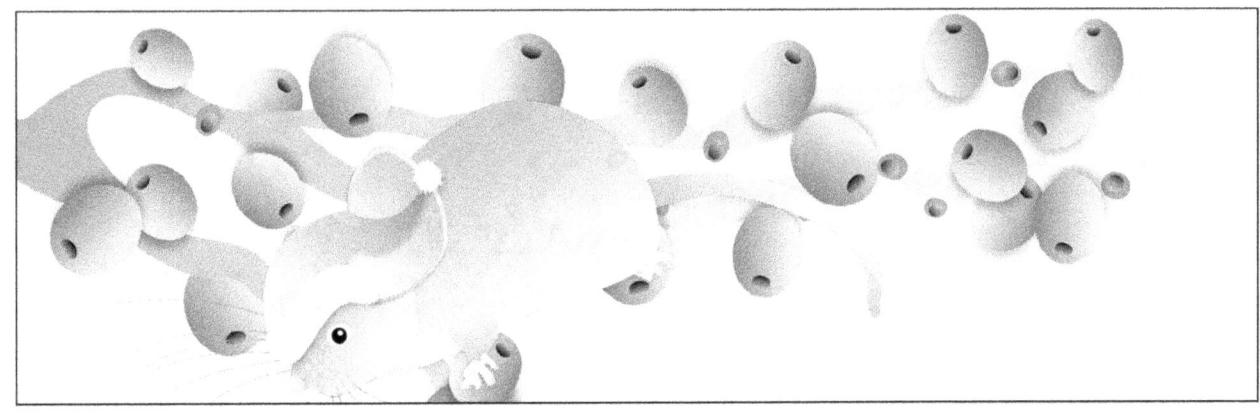

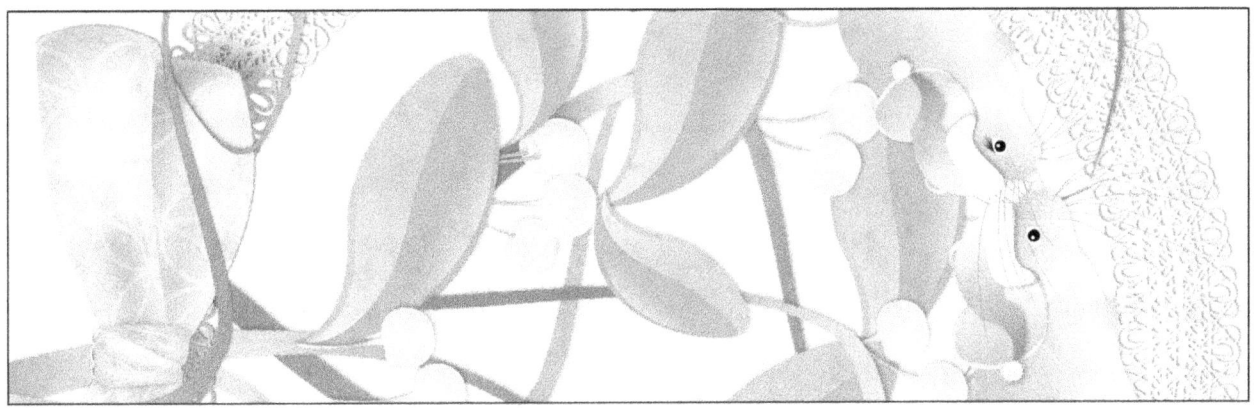

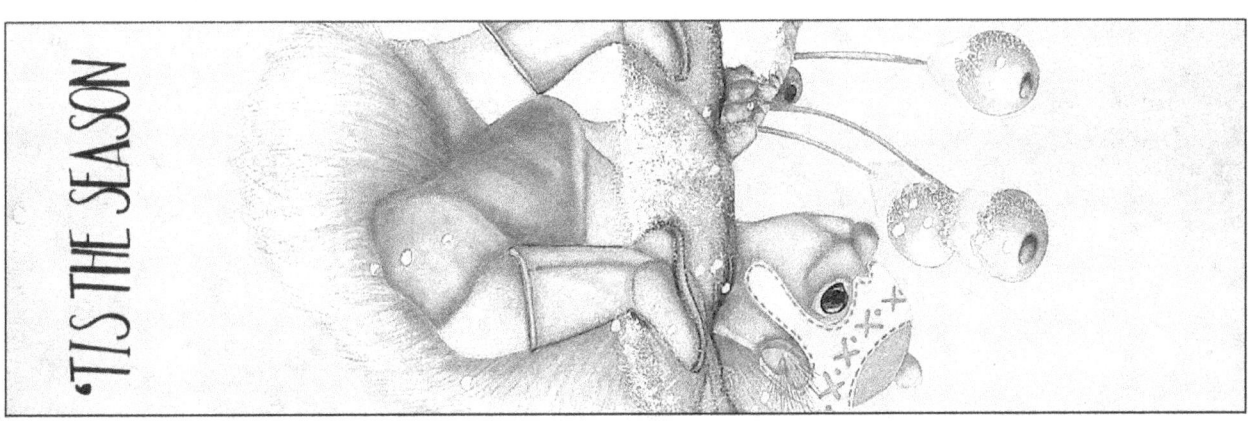

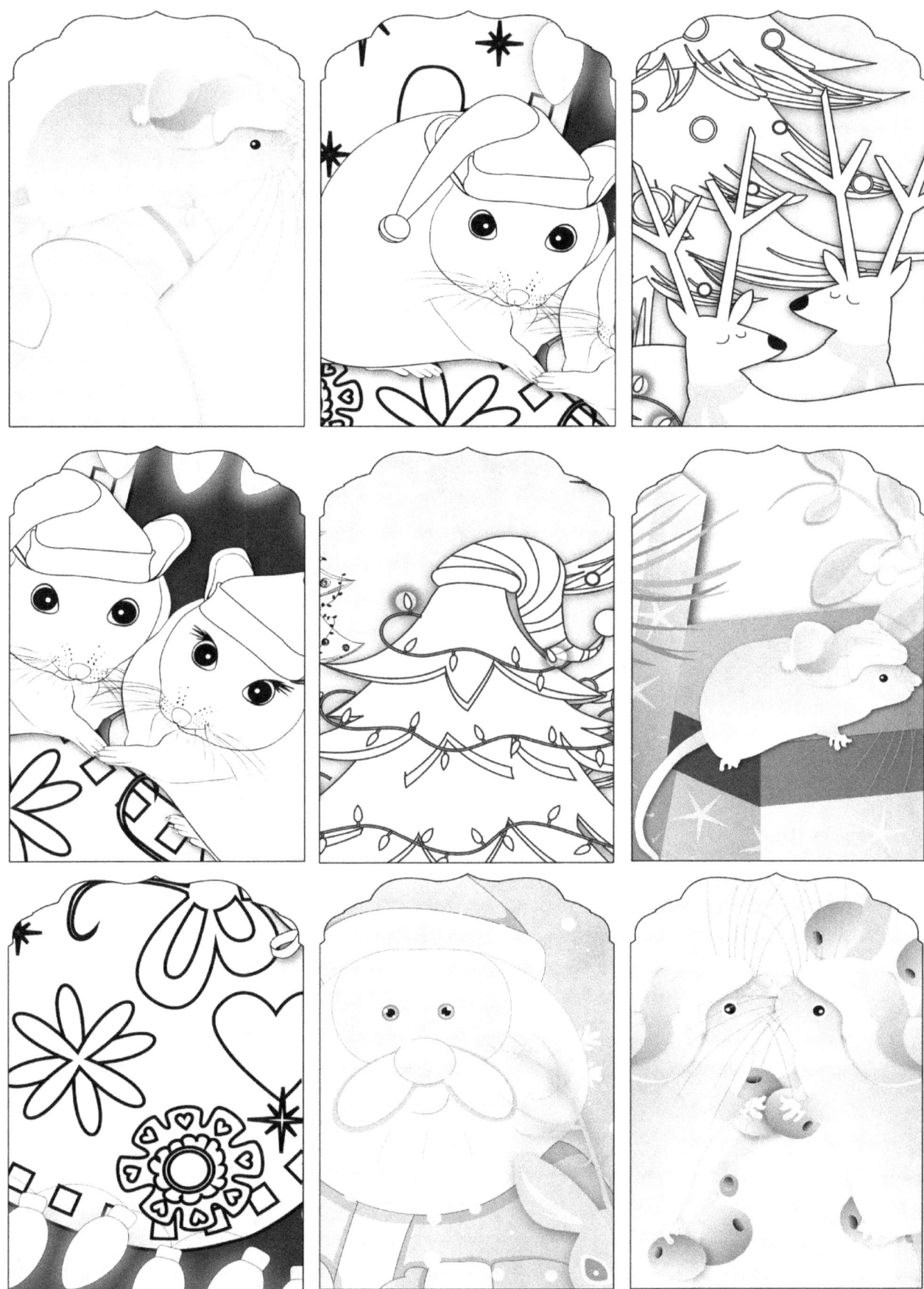

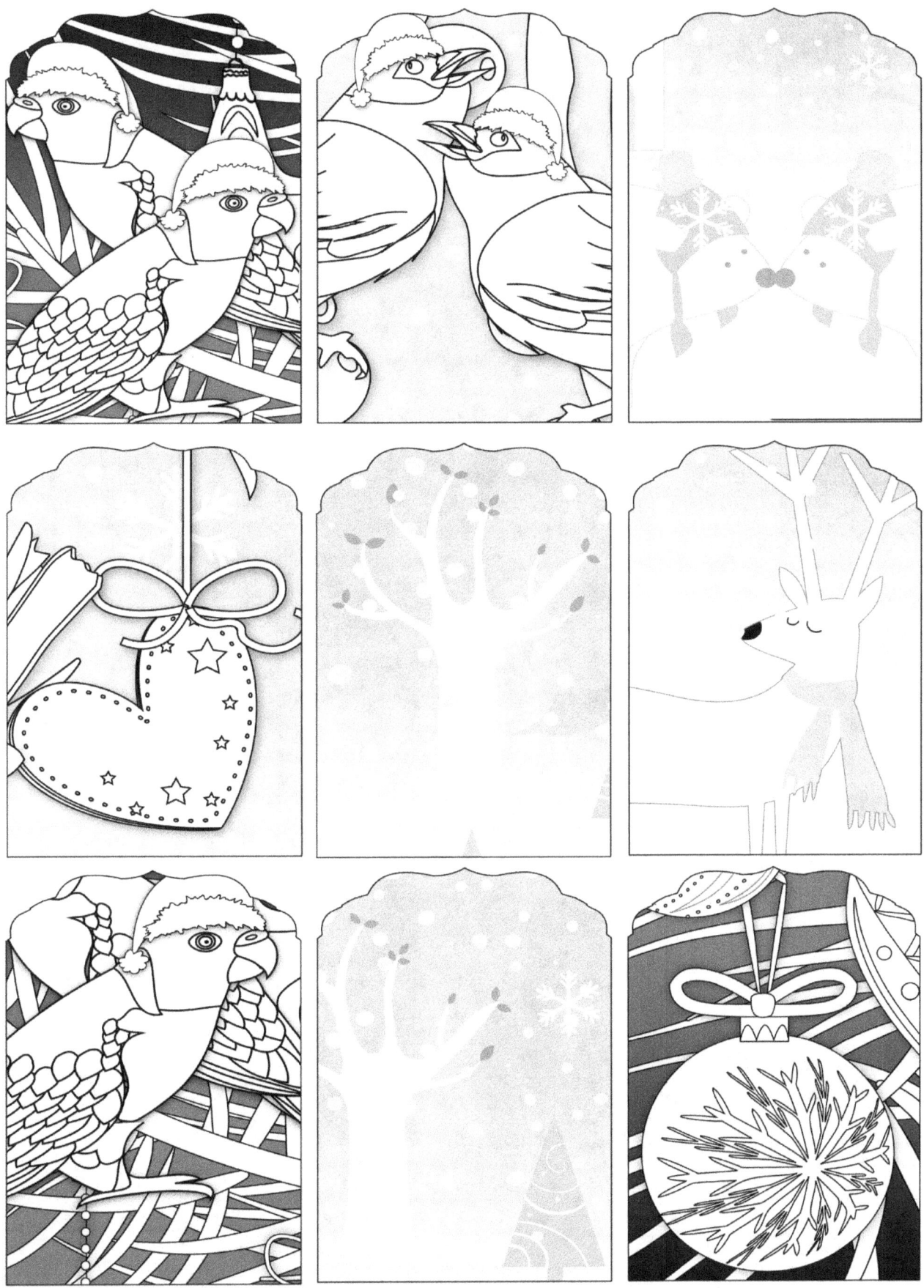

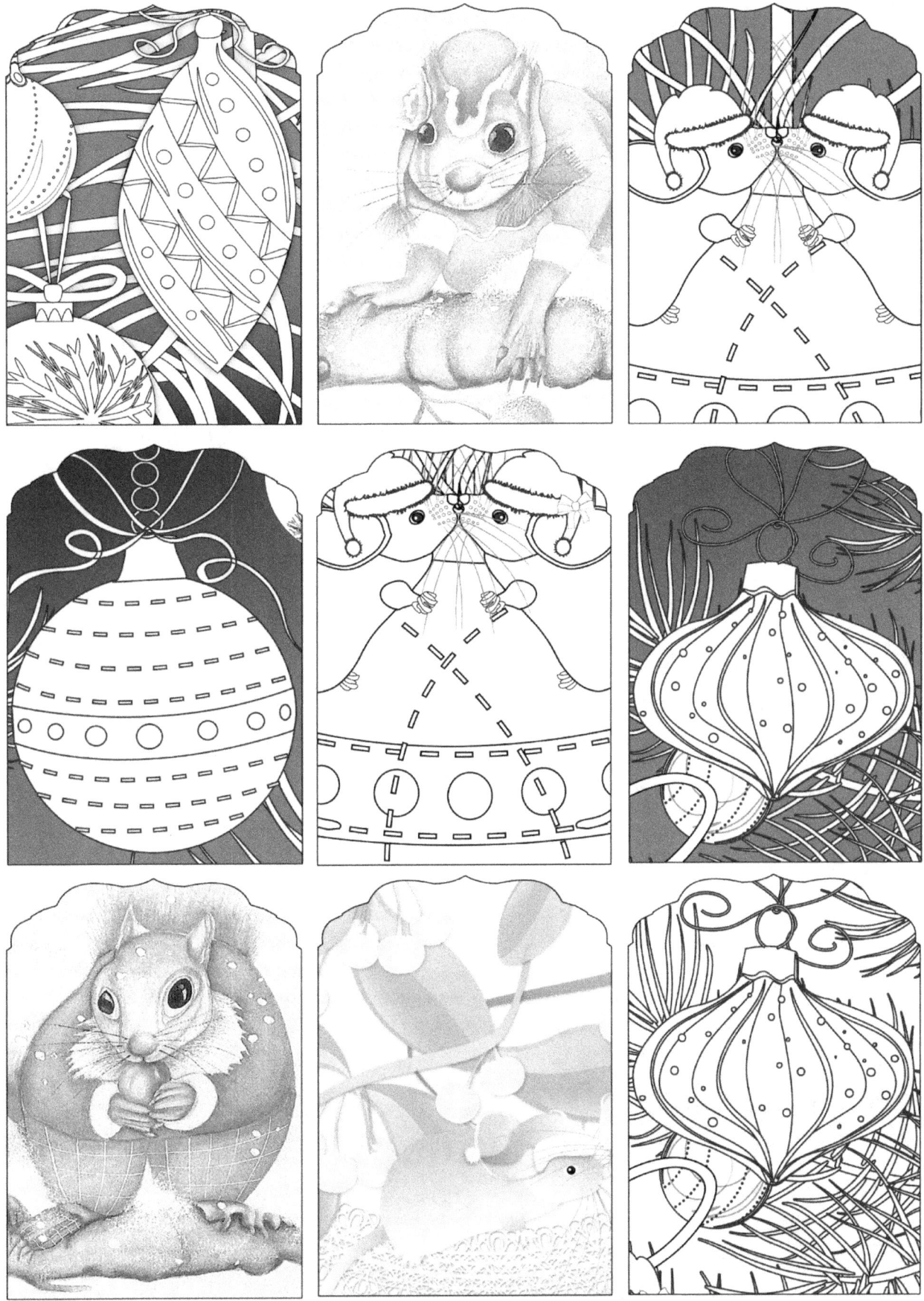

Have you seen my other Books on Amazon?

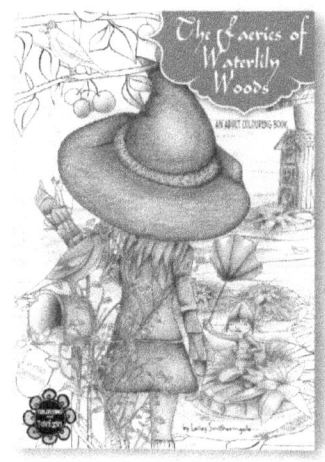

The Faeries of Waterlily Woods
Adult Colouring Book
- Line art Edition

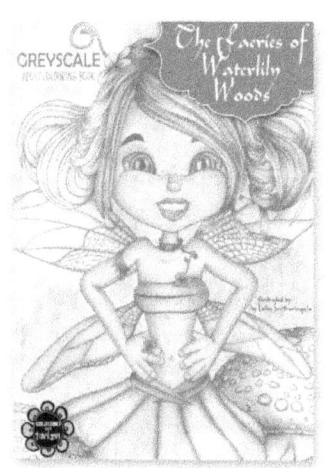

The Faeries of Waterlily Woods
Adult Colouring Book
- Greyscale Edition

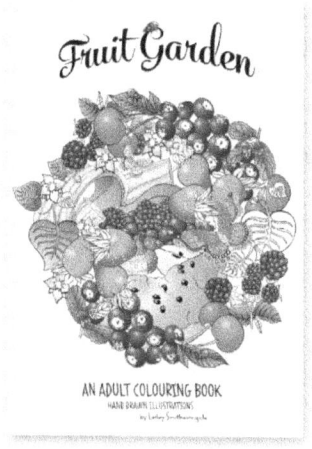

Fruit Garden
Adult Colouring Book

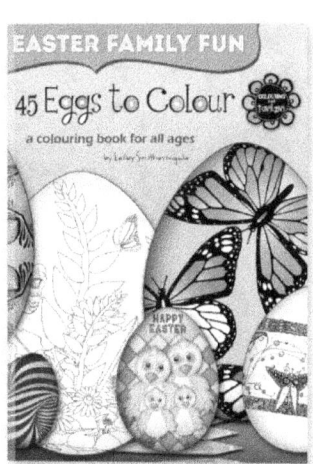

45 Eggs to Colour -
Easter Family Fun
Colouring Book for all Ages

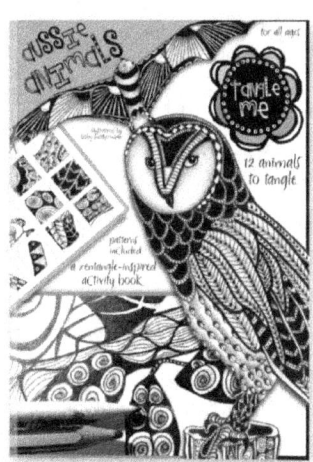

Tangle Me Aussie Animals -
a Zentangle-inspired
Activity Book for all Ages

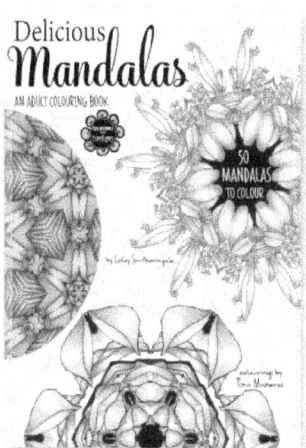

Delicious Mandalas
Adult Colouring Book

See them all on my Author Page on Amazon at

https://www.amazon.com/author/lesleysmitheringale